FAST LANE
to
HEAVEN

D0067032

NED DOUGHERTY

FAST LANE
to
HEAVEN

A Life-after-Death Journey

HAMPTON ROADS
PUBLISHING COMPANY, INC.

Copyright © 2001
by Ned Dougherty
All rights reserved, including the right to reproduce this
work in any form whatsoever, without permission
in writing from the publisher, except for brief passages
in connection with a review.

Cover design by Marjoram Productions
Cover art by PhotoDisc
For information write:

Hampton Roads Publishing Company, Inc.
1125 Stoney Ridge Road
Charlottesville, VA 22902

Or call: 434-296-2772
Fax: 434-296-5096
e-mail: hrpc@hrpub.com
www.hrpub.com

If you are unable to order this book from your local
bookseller, you may order directly from the publisher.
Call 1-800-766-8009, toll-free.
Library of Congress Catalog Card Number: 00-110247
ISBN 1-57174-336-7
10 9 8 7 6 5 4 3 2
Printed on acid-free paper in the United States

TO

THE LADY OF LIGHT

". . . Hear the pious prayer of all those who

recognize that yours is a reign of mercy, in

which every petition is heard, every sorrow

comforted, every misfortune relieved, every

infirmity healed, and in which, as a gesture

from your gentle hands, from death itself

there arises smiling life!"

AND TO

MICHAEL

In Her Words,

"Truly a son of God!"

TABLE OF CONTENTS

ACKNOWLEDGMENTS

The characters in this book are real, and the events are true, but I have used pseudonyms for several of the characters for privacy and other considerations. Although I was guided through my experience by only one of my friends, who had been killed in Vietnam, Lieutenant Daniel McCampbell is a pseudonym, and his character and the description of the events before his death represent the combined experiences of a number of my personal friends who had been killed or wounded, or who had served, in Vietnam. I owe a great debt of gratitude not only to these personal friends, but also to all of the brave men and women who served in Vietnam, particularly to those who sacrificed their lives, and who continue to inspire me from the Other Side.

I am also indebted to my friends in Alcoholics Anonymous for whom I have also used pseudonyms, especially to those both named and unnamed who traveled with me on the road to recovery—particularly George B., Paul G., Peter H., Ray H., Jimmy L., and, posthumously, Larry S.

For research material, personal meetings, and professional guidance, I relied on the consultation and advice of Bruce Greyson, M.D., University of

Virginia, Charlottesville, Virginia. I am personally indebted to Dr. Greyson for his encouragement and support, particularly during 1994 and 1995 when I embarked on the mission that resulted in this manuscript. Through his work and support as director of research for the International Association for Near-Death Studies (IANDS), Dr. Greyson has provided inspiration and support to thousands of near-death survivors throughout the world.

I would also like to thank several other professional consultants and/or "pioneers" in near-death research: P. M. H. Atwater, L.H.D.; Raymond A. Moody, Jr., M.D.; Melvin Morse, M.D.; Kenneth Ring, Ph.D.; George Ritchie, M.D.; Elisabeth Kübler-Ross, M.D.; Michael Sabom, M.D.; and Ian Stevenson, M.D.

During my two-year tenure on the Board of Directors of IANDS, I gratefully received the support and friendship of my fellow board members: Phyllis Atwater, Maggie Callanan, Diane Corcoran, Elizabeth Fenske, Bruce Horacek, Debbie James, Jo Ann Marnie, Leslee Morabito, Sandra Procko, and Karl Williamson. I am particularly grateful to IANDS past president Nancy Evans Bush for giving me the opportunity to serve as a board member. I have also been inspired by the work and friendship of John Van Auken, Dannion Brinkley, Mally Cox Chapman, Bill Guggenheim, Sarah Hinze, Betty Paraskevas, and Mickey Paraskevas.

My spiritual journey through life resulted in my meeting a number of spiritual leaders who had an ever-lasting impact on my life, particularly His Eminence Cardinal John O'Connor of New York, Monsignor Tom Hartman of The God Squad, and Mother Angelica. During the writing and editing of this manuscript I spent time in prayer and meditation at the following retreats and wish to extend thanks to all of the priests and brothers who were my gracious and inspiring hosts at the Montfort House at Lourdes of Litchfield, Connecticut; the Monastery of the Holy Spirit, Conyers, Georgia; the New Camaldoli Hermitage, Big Sur, California; and particularly to Father Bill, Father Ray, and Brother Chris at Our Lady of the Island Shrine, Eastport, New York. (My acknowledgement of these individuals and religious organizations should not be construed or misunderstood as an approval of this manuscript by any religious authority. This manuscript has not been read, reviewed, influenced, or in any way been given an *imprimatur* by any religious authority.)

A house fire in February 1998 destroyed most of my research material, personal diaries, much of the original manuscript, and a file of names of people whom I wished to acknowledge for contributions both great and small that enabled me to complete my work. I apologize if I failed to specifically mention your name here, if such promise had been made prior to the fire. However, your contributions are greatly appreciated—you know who you are!

As a novice writer, I relied on the encouragement and support of a number of friends and professional individuals who provided critical readings of the manuscript, with particular thanks to Professor Judy Sider O'Donnell for her editing work. I am also grateful to Gary Aumiller, Dave Brady, Rita Boettger, Peter Brennan, Bill Buonora, Mitch Douglas at ICM, Stephanie Evans, Ted and Maureen Flynn, Maureen Gaffney, Nancy Gershwin, Kathy Johnson, Tom Leahy, P. J. McKillop, Daryl McNicholas, Nicole Moniaci, Marie Mulcahy, Rhonda Riccio, Mary Lou Robinson, Betty Smith, Sarah Smith, Alexandra Teguis, Mary Terry, and Debbie Tuma. I would also like to thank Dr. Richard A. Blum,

University of Central Florida, and, posthumously, Professor Kay Weber, my English professor at St. John's University who encouraged me to pursue a career in writing—over thirty years ago.

I personally chose Hampton Roads Publishing Company as my publisher and wish to thank all of the Hampton Roads staff members who assisted in the preparation of Fast Lane to Heaven. I particularly wish to thank my editor, Richard Leviton, along with Rebecca Williamson, Kathy Cooper, Rebecca Whitney, Grace Pedalino, Jen Hummel, Anne Dunn, and most of all, Frank DeMarco and Bob Friedman.

Finally, I wish to thank the Brennan family; the Kearns family; and most of all—my mother, Isabelle; sister Kay; Ginnie, Jacob, and Michael.

PROLOGUE

AN HOA BASIN
SOUTH VIETNAM
May 31, 1969

> We say that the hour of death cannot be forecast,
> but when we say this we imagine that hour as
> placed in an obscure and distant future. It never
> occurs to us that it has any connection with the
> day already begun or that death could arrive this
> afternoon . . . this afternoon that is so certain and
> which has every hour filled in advance!
> —*Marcel Proust*

As the sun rose over the Que Son Mountains and
into An Hoa Basin on the morning of May 31, 1969, the
oppressive heat closed in on a U.S. Marine Corps platoon patrolling in the primitive tropical forest. The heat
had a way of affecting the men in the platoon and their
platoon leader, Lieutenant Daniel McCampbell.

Lieutenant McCampbell cautiously led his platoon
through the jungle, the heat sweltered around him,
attempting to alter his judgment, forcing him to make

mistakes, and increasing the risk for the men in his charge. He would be "in country" only twenty more days before returning home forever, or so he thought, and he was counting the hours, and the minutes, and the seconds. He was also thinking of home, but he had little time for that when he was responsible for the lives of his men in the jungle. Home was thousands of miles away from this God-forsaken place in the Republic of Vietnam.

Dan was on his second combat tour in Vietnam and well-prepared to be in charge of his platoon, part of an amphibious force assigned duties that required close and continuous support and contact with the local Vietnamese civilians and the South Vietnamese soldiers.

As a result of four years of combat training and two tours in Vietnam, Dan had developed a sixth sense that he believed had kept him and his men alive. His "street smart" sense had allowed him to survive in the asphalt jungle of his old neighborhood. But it was the Corps that gave him the training to fine-tune his instincts to survive the horror of war in the jungles of Southeast Asia.

He saw something on the trail ahead that stopped him in his tracks, and a dark feeling of foreboding came over him. Usually, he had responded to his instincts only from some external influence that signaled him to be more cautious. But this feeling that came over him now included something new; a feeling that was coming from someplace deeper within his soul, a feeling that left him with an overwhelming sense of dread.

Dan was convinced that danger lay ahead. The area was probably booby-trapped. What activated Dan's inner alarm were a North Vietnamese Army flag and an ammunition box lying on the trail in front of him. Dan signaled the platoon's grenadier to come forward. He positioned himself and his M-79 next to his lieutenant. Dan ordered the grenadier to launch a rifle grenade at both objects to detonate any hidden booby traps. The grenade landed near the objects and exploded as the platoon members crouched for cover. No secondary explosion was forthcoming.

Dan directed the grenadier to fire another grenade. This time the grenade landed on the ammunition box, rolled off, and exploded. The platoon members crouched and huddled in anticipation of a secondary explosion. A long pause, more than enough time, but the jungle was silent and still after the echoes of the exploding grenades disappeared. Certainly, no booby trap device could have survived such a shelling. The platoon members began to rise from their hiding places, collecting their gear, and preparing to examine their target.

Dan was organizing himself for an inspection of the target area and checking on his men, distracted for an instant, thinking again about going home, trying to dismiss that feeling of dread. A younger and less experienced member of the platoon passed behind Dan toward the target. Dan sensed the danger in the young recruit's movements and turned to the recruit to give a warning, assuming that the young Marine was going to make a fatal mistake and grab for the prized souvenirs.

Dan's instincts formed a thought in his mind: *"No, don't!"* But before that nanosecond of time from thought to speech could allow Dan to verbalize the warning, the young Marine moved behind him toward the target site. As Dan began to mouth the words, a bright flash of searing heat passed before and through him. A fragmentation device had exploded into jagged pieces of deadly metal, instantly killing the younger Marine.

As Lieutenant Daniel J. McCampbell witnessed the flash of brilliant light, the fragments were also exploding through his own body. Dan was already dead, killed instantly, before his lifeless body crumbled to the ground. Yet, he found himself hovering above and beyond the horrific scene, detached and floating free, viewing the remains of his own mutilated body. *"It wasn't supposed to be this way! This wasn't supposed to happen to me!"*

I know someone in Christ who—
fourteen years ago—whether in the body
or out of the body—I do not know, God knows,
was caught up into the third heaven. And I know
that this person—I do not know, God knows,
was caught up into Paradise
And heard ineffable
things, which no one
may utter!
2 Corinthians 12:2-4

INTRODUCTION

Death comes upon you when you least expect it. It comes over you quickly, and it lets you know it is present. Usually it comes with finality, as it did for my friend Dan McCampbell. But in my own case, I experienced the other side of existence that we call death, and I came back from death to tell you about it. Obviously, I came back—because here I am, breathing and writing. I am here most of the time anyway.

My first experience with "death" happened on the night of July 2, 1984. Since then, books, movies, and television documentaries have popularized the term "near-death experience" to describe an event that has been experienced by millions of people who have been at death's door. But back in 1984 I was alone with my experience. I couldn't share it with anyone.

Coming back from death is a powerful and life-changing experience. Before I came back from death, I was told that I was coming back with a mission in life. My mission was not clearly defined for me at first, but I now find that each and every day it is being defined for me more clearly. The experience has set me upon a path of self-discovery and spiritual enlightenment that continues to provide me with glimpses into the afterlife—glimpses that I would now like to share with you. Prior to finding myself at death's door, I was not by nature inclined to share anything with anybody, but now I believe it is important that I share my experiences with you.

Ned Dougherty

PART I

THE EXPERIENCE

"To die will be an awfully big adventure!"
—*J. M. Barrie*, Peter Pan

CHAPTER 1

THE HAMPTONS

Long Island, New York
July 2, 1984
The evening

HE WHO DIES WITH THE MOST TOYS WINS!
—*Popular Hamptons' bumper sticker*

I spent the early evening drinking champagne with friends at a luxurious contemporary home in Remsenburg, a quiet hamlet at the western end of the Town of Southampton. Actually I only had several glasses, maybe three or four; I was pacing myself because I wanted to be sharp and alert for the evening. It was the July Fourth vacation week, and I owned Club Marakesh, the most successful nightclub in the Hamptons, probably in all of New York.

I was looking forward to another successful evening. Club Marakesh attracted a diverse crowd, mostly from New York City. Celebrities, sports personalities, models, Wall Street brokers looking for models, lawyers, fashion people, advertising people, film and record executives, WASP socialites, trust-fund brats, Europeans, drug dealers, and Mafia mobsters. Everyone and anyone who came to the Hamptons wanted to get into Club Marakesh.

Every weekend, long lines of patrons would form along the front of the building behind velvet ropes waiting for the privilege to pay twenty or twenty-five dollars just to walk in the door to the already-overcrowded club. Even though some would wait for hours to get inside, I would arrogantly pick the "chosen ones" who were given the privilege to pass beyond the velvet ropes. Even VIP patrons and celebrities stood patiently in front of the velvet ropes until the maître d' indicated with a wave of his arm that their tables were ready.

Attractive waitresses earning summer money for college would serve chilled champagne in frosted glasses. Dom Perignon, Perrier Jouet, and Cristal were the favorites. Individual patrons at the tables spent hundreds—sometimes thousands—of dollars a night on champagne. Some of them even challenged each other to see who could spend the most.

I had every right to feel confident and arrogant. At the age of thirty-seven, I was single and having an affair with a very attractive waitress—blonde, beautiful, and only nineteen, approximately half my age. I had successfully avoided marriage and children. I did not want to be tied down by any woman, and I considered children to be a nuisance. I had a succession of girls, all blonde and all beautiful. None of my relationships lasted very long, and I liked it that way.

I grew up in a modest, middle-class neighborhood in Hazleton, a small city in northeastern Pennsylvania.

I left Hazleton after graduating from St. Gabriel's Catholic High School in 1964. I then attended St. John's University in New York City where I majored in parties and girls. Following a brief career on Wall Street, I moved to the Hamptons to party full-time after learning that I had successfully avoided military service and Vietnam. I became a real estate broker because I thought it was an easy way to make money and live independently in the Hamptons. Then I got into the nightclub business.

I opened Club Marakesh in the Hamptons in the summer of 1976 and created and built another Club Marakesh in West Palm Beach, Florida in 1978. Both clubs were enormously successful. I spent my summers in the Hamptons and my winters in Palm Beach. I had a luxurious contemporary home with a swimming pool in the Hamptons and apartments in both Palm Beach and Manhattan. I drove a Mercedes-Benz convertible and traveled by private jet, seaplane, helicopter, and limousine. I dined in the trendiest restaurants with celebrities and sports personalities, seated by maître d's at the best tables.

I was part of the Baby Boomer generation that set its goals on material comfort and success. Despite my religious upbringing as a Roman Catholic, I had no interest in a spiritual life because I didn't believe in an afterlife. I believed that life was over when it was over. I was neither agnostic nor atheistic. I was too busy searching for a good time to be bothered with such things. My motto was "He who dies with the most toys, wins!" And I had accumulated my share of toys. Nothing else mattered.

Although I lived an exciting, fun-filled life and had all the money and toys the world had to offer, my life was not without stress. My lifestyle and notoriety and the fact that I was in a high-profile cash business had not gone unnoticed by the Internal Revenue Service. In fact, I was the subject of a three-year probe for income-tax evasion with accusations of money laundering in offshore banks.

The allegations that were being made by the treasury agents who were investigating the case were preposterous and were based largely on guilt by association. In both New York and Florida, I socialized with various disreputable characters at my nightclubs, many of whom may have been involved in various illegal activities, but I was not involved in their activities. Several federal agencies, including the IRS, the FBI, and the DEA, thought differently. In the collective eyes of these agencies, I was a typical nightclub owner, a fantasy role created by agents who watched too many Hollywood movies.

Federal agents regularly patronized my nightclubs following the characters who were under surveillance. This was very good for business. Even agents had to pay the cover charges as well as pay for their drinks. Whenever I was observed sitting at a table in one of my clubs with suspected characters, I would be presumed to be involved in their illegal activities. In reality, my nightclub businesses were managed like banks, and I kept meticulous business records. I believed there was no reason to compromise my legitimate business activities. Certainly I would have relished the adrenaline rush of being involved in dangerous pursuits, but I didn't want to jeopardize what I already had.

Unfortunately, one of my business associates in the late 1970s had made the mistake of talking to members of a Mafia organized crime family about investing in a large nightclub that we intended to open in Times Square. This guilt by association triggered a federal focus on my business interests that was still ongoing in 1984.

After a series of threats and intimidation from this crime family, we walked away from the Times Square deal with a considerable loss of money. It was the first time I had ever lost in a business deal. Adding insult to injury, my associate and I developed the reputation, as a result of rumors and speculation, of being mobbed-up, meaning that we were owned or controlled by the Mafia. I never forgave this business associate and blamed him for our losses and for courting a relationship with Mafia wiseguys in the first place. Although this incident had taken place five years earlier, I continued to have resentments toward this business associate.

As I sat talking and drinking champagne with my friends Bill and Mary Lou at their home, those old resentments started to surface again because of an incident that had happened early that morning. The same business associate had been arrested for possession of a substantial amount of cocaine.

It didn't bother me that he had the cocaine; it bothered me that he got caught with it. Cocaine was a very important part of the nightclub scene; cocaine and champagne went together. Almost everyone I knew from the Hamptons to Manhattan to Palm Beach used cocaine, regardless of their profession or occupation. They were all part of an elite and wealthy nightclub sub-culture.

It didn't help matters that Bill and Mary Lou were openly expressing their concern that the arrest of this business associate could have enormous repercussions on my business interests. None of my business associates had ever been arrested before, and the nature of these charges was certain to have an impact with the current federal investigation. As I sat listening to my friends' concerns, I was already projecting a number of unfortunate scenarios as a result of this arrest.

Although I tried to maintain my composure, years of resentment were seething inside me.

My friends and I decided to go to dinner at a restaurant across the street from Club Marakesh before going to the club. As we drove the several miles from Remsenburg to the village, I had time to reflect on the situation, and the more I thought about it, the angrier I became. Although I had had a bad temper as a kid, I had learned to control it over the years. I tried to relax as we drove back to the village, but I felt strong surges of adrenaline pumping into my system. These surges of adrenaline were stronger than I had ever felt before, but the adrenaline rush was certainly not warranted, despite the rage I was feeling. Perhaps I was being prepared for the worst possible scenario.

Holiday weekends in the Hamptons meant even less sleep than usual, and I had been running in overdrive physically for three days and nights. As I continued to feel more uneasy, I recognized that I was operating on a lot of nervous energy. When I allowed myself to get this stressed out, I would usually burn out and crash for a day or so. But it was evening—Show Time—and another opening night at Marakesh. Despite my inner turmoil, I thought I would get through the night at the club and try to get some serious sleep in the morning.

As we drove onto Main Street in the village, I became more energized and felt more in control of myself when I saw how crowded the village was. The village's Main Street consisted of three short blocks of restaurants, boutiques, art galleries, ice cream stores, and real estate offices. The Club Marakesh building was, by far, the most prominent building on the street. The charming tree-lined street was jam-packed with holiday traffic, and throngs of people were crowding the sidewalks, guaranteeing yet another busy night at Marakesh.

I agreed to meet my friends at the restaurant after doing a walk-through tour of Marakesh and checking up on the employees who were preparing the club for opening. I thought that the business associate, who had already been released on bail, would have enough sense to lie low for a couple of days after his arrest. Knowing that I would not have to deal with him personally, I started feeling even better as I approached the club.

Several of the club's security personnel were setting up the stanchions and velvet ropes on the sidewalk in preparation for the night's crowd. I walked into the front lobby and climbed the stairwell that led to the private VIP lounge that overlooked the main level and dance floor of the club. From my vantage point in the VIP room, I could look out over the rest of the club and decide how the staff was performing. Although the VIP room was relatively dark and quiet, I sensed that someone else was in the room. It was the business associate who was the focus of my rage. He began shouting as he walked toward me with a drink in one hand, while pointing a finger at me with the other. I didn't even listen to what he was saying. I just exploded; I leapt at him with a volley of fists, knocking him backwards. As he stumbled and fell, I lunged at him with both hands in a death-like grip around his neck. My instincts, fueled by rage, were murderous. As he grasped for breath, I squeezed harder, recognizing that I could easily resolve this business association by pressing my thumb further into the vulnerable spot at the center of his throat. As I seriously contemplated actually murdering him, something happened inside me that I didn't expect. I couldn't force my thumb to sink further into his neck to cause more severe or even fatal damage.

As I recognized that some invisible force was holding me back, I realized that some other, evil force had overwhelmed me only moments before to the point that I was actually contemplating murdering someone and, in a moment of madness, had assumed that the murder would somehow be justified. For someone who took pride in maintaining control and being patient, my explosive reaction in this situation was as much a surprise to me as it was to the employees who overheard the commotion.

At that moment, when my uncontrolled and violent attempt to commit murder was abated by an inner voice, another force in the form of a security guard grabbed me in a body-hold from behind and pulled me away from the object of my rage. I was as startled by the inner voice that had stopped me from committing murder as I was by the security guard's intervention. For several seconds, as I was being pulled back from my intended prey, I realized that only a few seconds and an unforeseen force had kept me from committing murder and possibly spending the rest of my life in prison.

The security guard, probably as startled by his own response as he was to the unreality of the situation, persuaded me to go back downstairs. As I stumbled down the stairs to the front lobby, I concentrated on calming myself. I was gasping for air and trying to control my breathing. I soon realized that my lungs were hyperventilating out of control. My chest seemed to be expanding and contracting more and more rapidly, but with each expansion and contraction, less oxygen was reaching my lungs. I could hear my heart pounding heavily in my chest.

As I walked out of the front lobby onto the sidewalk, I passed the security guards and employees at the entrance who were unaware of the explosive incident that had just taken place in the VIP room. I was walking alone now, still trying desperately to catch my breath as I stumbled into an alleyway. I spotted my friend Bill and suddenly realized that something was seriously wrong. Alarms were going off inside my head, but just as suddenly I felt surrounded by a warm and secure feeling, despite the fact that I felt that I was no longer in control of what was physically happening to me. For the first time in many years, I shot a glance up into the dark sky above me as if I was reaching to heaven to come to my aid. The warm and secure feeling that I was experiencing must have been coming from someplace other than from inside because what was going on physically within my body was creating terror and trauma in my mind.

As Bill met me, I tried to tell him I needed help, but it was too late. Although my uncontrolled hyperventilating had ceased, so did my breathing. Time and space stood still. My sense of hearing turned inward, and I was listening for sounds from my now-silent lungs, which seemed to have collapsed. Just seconds ago my heart had been pounding loudly and now, suddenly, the pounding stopped. For a long pregnant moment, everything before me stood still. I was dying and I knew it. In a split second, I thought: *This is it! This is how it all ends!* Suddenly, I felt what seemed like an electrical explosion in my head, and my body collapsed to the sidewalk.

CHAPTER 2

THE DESCENT

July 2, 1984, 10:20 P.M.

As my lifeless body hit the sidewalk, I consciously continued to fall without my physical body. It felt as if I had fallen through the sidewalk, or that the sidewalk had opened up below me, and I was consciously falling into an abandoned well without my body. I was looking up toward a beam of light that I perceived to be the hole in the sidewalk. As I continued to fall more and more rapidly, the beam of light became smaller and smaller until it was only a pin dot. Like a distant star, it diminished, and then it was gone as I continued to fall into total blackness.

It was like falling down an elevator shaft or into a cavern, but it was totally dark. As I continued to fall, I realized that it was not my physical body that was falling into this black void. I was fully conscious and mentally alert. I recognized that I was actually in a state of consciousness, devoid of any physical reality or form. It was not me in a physical body or in any form of physical state that was falling; it was me as a conscious being. It did not upset me that I no longer had a physical form or that I was out of my body, but I was upset, even terrorized, by the condition of my falling.

Then my descent began to decelerate, and I found myself slowing down and then floating, suspended in a black, bottomless pit, in a dark and heavy void. I was alone, without physical form, in darkness, suspended in complete and dark nothingness. Despite being fully awake and alert, I had no way of groping in the darkness since I had no physical form. I was trapped in a conscious state with no ability to extricate myself from this darkness. If I had my body, I could possibly feel the bottom of this pit with my arms and legs, or maybe crawl to a side wall and pull myself back up. But to where? From where? In what form?

As I realized that my options were limited, I sensed that my ability to create further options was diminishing. I could no longer be creative in removing myself from this place or situation. A horrible feeling of terror and panic started to overwhelm me. I had no control over my situation. I was alone and had no one to turn to. I thought, *Who could I turn to at this moment?* Inexplicably, I then thought of someone that I had put out of my life for a long time. I thought about God.

Suddenly, a new sense of awareness came over me. I sensed that the beam of light from which I had fallen was somehow representative of the only opportunity I had to rescue myself. The beam of light, I thought, emanated from God, the Creator, and from Creation itself. And with that thought in mind, I became aware that in my conscious mind I was calling upon a knowledge state that had been long dormant, residing deep within my subconscious.

13

Calling upon this reawakened knowledge, I recognized that the beam of light from which I had fallen into this darkness was the light of God, the Creator. Therefore, I was in a most hapless and helpless state, since I had fallen so far from Him. I was, it seemed, as far from the Creator as one could get and still exist. Since God was the Creator and Creation itself, and the light of creation emanated from God, I was as far away from God as I could be, for I was in a black, bottomless void in total darkness.

I knew instinctively in which direction I wanted to go. I wanted to go toward the light, but the light was gone. I didn't want to think of remaining in this black hole. I sensed that if I fell any further, I would no longer exist. I would just simply cease to exist. A period of time went by. I could not tell how long I had been in the dark void. I could not tell if it had been seconds or an eternity. I was not capable of measuring time in this void; nor was I capable of measuring space. My ability to create thought, to be cognitive, and to think was rapidly diminishing. I no longer had any options as the place I was in became more oppressive and suffocating. I was reduced to the lowest level in existence as far as I could tell.

A feeling of claustrophobic fear gripped me, and I had only one thought in mind—but then even the fear disappeared, and I was no longer capable of feeling or expressing emotion. I kept repeating the only thought my mind was capable of generating. *I am! . . . I am! . . . I am!* I repeated it in order to survive, over and over, as if the very thought was the pulse of my consciousness that allowed me to continue to exist.

I am! . . . I am! . . . I am!

CHAPTER 3

THE AMBULANCE TRIP

July 2, 1984, 10:30 P.M.

Meanwhile, Bill and Mary Lou and a crowd of people gathered around my lifeless body as it lay on the ground in the alleyway. Bill was the first person to kneel at my side. As he examined my body, he watched my complexion turn blue then gray. My breathing had stopped, and he could not get a pulse. I had no vital signs. No heartbeat. I was dead.

Bill was a very gifted carpenter, mechanic, and fisherman. He had built the Palm Beach club for me and was currently doing renovations at the Hamptons club. Now, as he knelt at my side, he was going to have to save my life. He began to administer CPR, pounding on my chest while giving mouth-to-mouth resuscitation, but my body was not responding. He continued the resuscitation procedures, but my lungs did not respond. He continued mouth-to-mouth resuscitation, still trying to get a response.

Several police officers arrived on the scene and radioed for an ambulance. The ambulance dispatcher received the call at 10:26 P.M. and immediately relayed a message to a nearby ambulance crew that an unconscious male was located in the alleyway next to Club Marakesh. Fortunately, the ambulance crew was less than a block away responding to another call that turned out to be a false alarm. They immediately proceeded to the scene in the alleyway, arriving at 10:27 P.M.

The crew quickly wheeled their gurney into the crowd of policemen, friends, and pedestrians who had gathered at the scene. The emergency medical technicians immediately recognized that their patient was unconscious, unresponsive, and in respiratory arrest, so they performed a "scoop and run"—getting their patient on the gurney, into the ambulance, and to the hospital as soon as possible. They moved with lightning speed as my body was transported into the ambulance, and the EMTs began procedures to resuscitate and stabilize me. Bill jumped into the front seat of the ambulance next to the driver.

As the ambulance sped from the scene and the crowd began to disperse, the policemen lingered for a few minutes discussing what had taken place, and whether or not it looked like I was going to make it. One of the policemen was carrying a handheld transmitter-receiver that was on the same frequency as the ambulance, now headed toward the hospital.

The policemen could overhear a play-by-play account of the activities in the ambulance. They could tell by the conversation between the ambulance driver and the hospital that things were not going well. Suddenly, while the policemen were discussing my odds of survival, they heard a sharp report from their two-way radio. It was the ambulance driver communicating to the hospital that the patient had just "coded." It looked like I wasn't going to make it.

Far, far away in the distance, I thought I could hear voices. I struggled and strained to listen, to make contact, with anyone. I was still immersed in total darkness, in a dark and heavy void. Silence and stillness. Then, far off again, I could hear voices. I began to float up, slowly but surely, drawn to the sounds that were still in the distance. . . .

"I have no vitals! We're losing him!"

I was startled when I heard those words. I tried to lift my head up to see what all the commotion was about. I was flat on my back in some ambulance. I felt my face fall off to my left side and come to rest on my shoulder as I lifted myself up to focus on an emergency medical technician who was sitting at my side. I was facing the EMT, but when I tried to tell him that everything was okay, he didn't seem to hear or notice me. He was looking right through me as if I wasn't even there.

There was a lot of commotion at this point, which I didn't understand. I was sitting up and felt fine, but the driver was accelerating the ambulance while talking into a two-way radio. He was announcing to the hospital that the patient had just "coded." I heard Bill shouting. "No, don't give up! You've got to make it! Hold on! Please, God, no!" Instinctively, I looked down at the gurney. The EMTs were working feverishly on a patient who appeared to be dead. Then I realized that the patient on the gurney was me.

I felt the ambulance slow down as the driver braked to execute a turn at a fork in the road. But as the ambulance proceeded forward and accelerated rapidly, I found myself catapulted through the roof and suspended in midair, watching the ambulance move rapidly down the dark wooded roadway, lights flashing, into the distance.

It took me several seconds to understand this new predicament. I was hovering in midair, suspended maybe forty or fifty feet above the road. As I tried to regain my composure, I looked down and noticed that my Rolex watch was missing. I focused my vision on the ambulance, disappearing in the distance. Those guys in the ambulance just stole my Rolex watch . . . and my money, and my clothes too. I tried again to regain my bearings when I also realized something else was missing—my body.

I looked down the dark road again. The ambulance was long gone now and along with it my body. I began to think I was the victim of some kind of scam that was far beyond my ability to comprehend. I was suspended in midair on a dark and lonely road with no Rolex watch, no money, no clothes, and no body.

This somehow seemed normal, but then something really strange happened. I found myself suspended in a state of consciousness watching a kaleidoscopic review of all the possessions and "toys" in my life. In rapid succession, I watched as all of these things passed by me and disappeared: the real estate, homes, Mercedes-Benz, helicopters, seaplanes, limousines—all disappearing into nothingness as if they had somehow been vaporized into nonexistence. I saw my first car from high school days and then my basketball, tennis racket, bicycle, and all of my toys going back to early childhood. I momentarily found myself standing in my grandmother's basement as a small boy watching my Lionel trains going around the track. Then the entire scene vaporized. I was still suspended over the highway, alone, my toys gone.

My attention was drawn to a brilliant starlit sky. I confidently gazed at a particular grouping of stars and instinctively, but inexplicably, thought, "I'm going home!"

As a massive field of energy began to form in the sky directly in front of me, I heard a loud, grinding mechanical noise as the mass of energy shaped itself into a cylinder funneling upwards. It seemed as if the darkness of the sky turned into liquid as the mass of energy curled like an ocean wave and formed a perfect tunnel that stretched into the heavens.

As I stared into the large and imposing tunnel of energy, a shimmering, luminescent-blue field of energy began to float down the tunnel toward me. As it rapidly approached, I watched the luminescent-blue field mass into a form and begin to materialize into an image of a human being. As the image composed itself, I found myself face-to-face with an old friend. His name was Dan McCampbell, but I had never expected to see him again. After all, he had been killed in Vietnam.

CHAPTER 4

THE ASCENT TO THE LIGHT

July 2, 1984, 10:37 P.M.

"Dan, I recognize you! You were killed in Vietnam! What are you doing here?"

"Relax, everything is okay!" Dan communicated to me with his engaging smile. "I'm here to show you the way!"

I had to adjust quickly to the new reality that now surrounded me. I was overwhelmed by the appearance of my friend who was smiling at me and conveying to me that everything is okay. Dan appeared to be young and very healthy, but his body was lighter, more ethereal than a human body. He appeared to be wearing combat fatigues that he would have worn in Vietnam.

As Dan and I communicated, I realized that we did not speak to each other as we had communicated in our earthly lives. As soon as I thought *Dan, I recognize you,* it was communicated to him. We were communicating telepathically, which connotes a communication of words between minds by means other than by vocal communication, but such a description falls short of the spiritual communication we were experiencing. We were not only communicating with words; we were communicating with feelings and emotions. As we thought, we also emoted our thoughts. Both thoughts and emotions were being communicated telepathically and spiritually in a manner that far surpassed normal human communication.

Dan communicated to me, "You are on the threshold of an important journey. Each of these places and events that are before you are for you to absorb as much as you can. It is important that you remember everything that you see before you. You will be going back, and you must go back with what you experience. You have a mission ahead of you in your life, and this experience will guide you on that mission."

As Dan and I communicated, we were suspended motionless in front of the energy tunnel. As Dan communicated that it was time to move on, my attention refocused on the tunnel. Dan led me toward the tunnel, and his presence was to my left as we moved forward.

I realized that I was comfortable with the fact that I had an ethereal human form but not a material body. I recognized that my being was in a natural state of existence, free of the limitations of the human body. I did not miss my human body and realized what a hindrance it was to be imprisoned in one.

As we moved forward into the tunnel, I recognized that I was moving forward by free will and not by appendages. No arms, legs, or other devices were required to obtain movement. I simply thought to move forward; I willed it, and the movement was accomplished. In an earthly sense, I felt more like a dolphin in water than a human on land. As we entered the tunnel of energy, I heard a loud and continuous whooshing sound surrounding us, and I felt as if we were entering a vacuum, except I heard, very sharply and clearly, the melodious sound of chimes and crystals and other wonderful—but unearthly—sounds.

I focused my attention on the composition of the walls of the tunnel as we moved forward. They resembled a massive ocean wave in a tubular form. My curiosity caused me to reach out in the direction of the wall to my right. As I touched its essence, a profusion of crystal-like liquid sparks danced and exploded in brilliant colors. The sparks of bright light were accompanied by the synchronous sounds of crystal-like chimes.

I was already hearing the melodious sounds of crystals and chimes from the time we entered the tunnel. This new profusion of sounds, caused by my disturbing the energy, should have clashed with the other sounds; but the new pattern of sounds complemented and intensified that continuous melody. This composition of sounds was far beyond the ability of any human composer to create.

I realized that my disturbing the energy field in the wall of the tunnel was easily absorbed by the power and energy responsible for the tunnel. Dan and I were traveling through a vehicle of energy that was so simple yet so complex that its nature was beyond description.

I turned back to Dan and communicated my wonderment at what I was experiencing. If I had to communicate my thoughts by words, I would have been speechless. I communicated that thought also and Dan understood. I was experiencing the ineffable.

"Relax, everything is okay," he repeated. "Trust the experience."

My attention was then drawn to the magnitude of the tunnel. At the distant opening before us, I could see

a universe of brilliant stars. I pondered the purpose of
the tunnel. It seemed to stretch from Earth into the universe for a distance measured in light years. We seemed
to be traveling very slowly through the tunnel although
we were moving through incredible distances in space.
It seemed as if the tunnel of energy reduced the distance
between Earth and our destination. It was as if we were
traveling up an escalator at a forty-five-degree angle at
the speed that an escalator would normally move in a
department store, yet we were moving through light
years of space in a matter of minutes. It was obvious
that the restrictions of mass, time, and space, as they
were measured in the physical world, did not apply in
the ethereal realm through which we were traveling.
Dan and I were not limited by them.

The tunnel of energy served several purposes. It was
a mass of energy that directed and assisted our travel. It
was a creation designed to contain us in an environment in which we felt comfortable and secure as we
traveled at an enormous speed through incredible distances in a very short period.

Suddenly, we exited the tunnel and were suspended
in a universe of bright stars. We were still moving
forward in this environment as if we were astronauts
propelled through space, but unencumbered by space
suits. We were moving like angels without wings. Dan
was still guiding me. I looked back and noticed that the
tunnel of energy was no longer visible. Instead, I was
looking deep into a void of space. I knew Earth was in
the direction from which we had come, but the planet
was now just a speck of light among a million stars.

I turned back to ask Dan if we had really traveled so far
that Earth was no longer identifiable, but he was no longer
at my side. As I began to turn forward again, I sensed a brilliant light approaching me. It seemed as if this powerful

light was rolling through the universe, engulfing the black void of space and all the stars and planets in its path.

Suddenly, I was enveloped in this brilliant golden light. The light was more brilliant than the light emanating from the Sun, many times more powerful and radiant than the Sun itself. Yet I was not blinded by it nor was I burned by it. Instead, the light was a source of energy that embraced my being.

I was alone in the glow of this light and suspended before a magnificent presence. I immediately believed that I was in the presence of God, my Creator. I felt that God was embracing me, and He had love for me, a love greater than any love I had ever known on earth. I realized that God was bestowing His light of love on me, as His light transformed from a brilliant golden light to a pure white light. As I became more accepting of God's love, the light of God became brighter, of a pure whiteness beyond description.

As the light of God's love was bestowed upon me, I felt it penetrate the top of my head and move down through my spirit body. As I was embraced by God's love, I saw microscopic particles of light radiating through my being. The more I focused on my acceptance of God's love, the brighter the light became as it vibrated and pulsated through my spiritual being, transforming itself continuously from a brilliant golden color to pure whiteness. As God's love radiated through me, it removed all the pain and suffering that I remembered from my existence as a human. I felt that God was bestowing His love upon me as a cleansing and purification of my spirit. Despite all my faults and transgressions, I was being embraced by God. I realized that I was at home in His presence and that my journey as a human had been a learning experience away from God. Now that I was again in His presence, I felt reborn.

When I sensed that my spiritual being had received God's love to the point of overflowing, I became aware that God was stabilizing and energizing my being in preparation for my mission. I realized that I would be returning to my earthly life and that God was preparing and orienting me for that return.

God began to imbue me with universal knowledge. I realized that I had always thirsted for this knowledge and I wanted to absorb as much as I could. As I remained suspended in God's light, I felt this knowledge penetrate and become absorbed by my spiritual being. This knowledge was flowing through me in the same manner as God's love, pulsating through my being.

As I became more receptive to the idea that I was in God's presence, He became more available to me. He was infinitely wise and knew everything about me. He knew that I wanted to know where I had gone wrong, and He showed me. He showed me that I had stopped searching for universal knowledge, and that I had blinded myself to my origin and to the meaning of my existence. He allowed me to realize that I had reduced myself to the point that I believed my existence ended upon my physical death. Therefore, I had no reason to search for universal knowledge. Now that I was again in God's presence, I realized that I was a spiritual being and that I was bestowed with God's gift of eternal existence. Imbued with the essence of God's light and love, I was exhilarated and filled with joy at the rediscovery of my true nature. Overflowing with feelings, I found myself expressing my first thoughts in recognition of the awareness that God was bestowing upon me.

"I am! I am! I am! I am a spiritual being!"

CHAPTER 5

SPIRITUAL REVELATIONS

Behold, I have opened a door for
you which cannot be shut!

Revelation 3:8

While in the presence of God's light, many revelations were conveyed to me. As God was bestowing a radiant energy upon me, I recognized that the energy contained information about universal laws, revelations that were part of God's plan for the universe.

I recognized that I could not possibly absorb and remember all of the knowledge for immediate recall, but I was aware that I would be able to call upon it in the future when it became necessary. Although the capacity of my memory was unlimited, my ability to process so much knowledge would be limited as a human being when I returned to Earth. My return to my earthly life would involve a forgetting as well as an awakening.

For a period of time, I remained suspended in the presence of God's light and love. I was surrounded by a radiant golden energy that emanated from the source I continued to recognize as God, the Creator. As the radiant energy filled me with universal knowledge, I was content to continue to absorb the knowledge that was being conveyed to me in waves of energy. In one respect, I felt that I was embarking on the dawn of a new era of existence. I felt as if the knowledge conveyed to me was a reorientation to truths that I had possessed previously, but that I had forgotten in my life.

As this process of absorbing knowledge was taking place, I was suspended in an upright position, alone, in God's presence. I could see the golden light radiating toward me from God. I felt as if I was in a graduation ceremony, departing from an existence of relative darkness and ignorance into a place of supreme light and enlightenment. I felt an incredible craving for this light and knowledge. I felt myself responding eagerly to the gifts that were being bestowed upon me by the Creator.

I recognized that I had always thirsted for this knowledge, especially during my youth, but in my search for a positive light on Earth I had ventured into a negative spiritual path as I grew older. I could not be sure if I actually and consciously pursued a negative path instead of a positive path or simply allowed myself to fall away from God. Instead of searching for the light through a spiritual journey, I chose to quench my thirst by pursuing pleasure through material possessions, sex, drugs, and alcohol. I had ventured onto a dark roadway of hedonistic pleasures and spiritual emptiness.

As I remained suspended before my Creator, willingly accepting His light, love, and knowledge, I realized that my earthly cravings, which had taken a negative turn, were appetites intended to be satisfied by following a spiritual path to enlightenment.

In my life, I awoke each day with a craving in the pit of my stomach, an emptiness that needed to be filled. I realized in God's presence that my solution to filling that craving was drinking. I had become addicted to alcohol in search of a solution to ending the craving.

But in God's presence, I realized that this craving was to be processed as a part of my spiritual journey, a journey which was now intended to be turned into a positive path in search of enlightenment. I had previously chosen a negative path in an attempt to somehow achieve positive results. This realization brought me to an understanding of the universal laws concerning the positive and negative forces of nature and allowed me to prepare myself to understand the gifts that God was bestowing upon me while I was in the light. God allowed me to see the positive side of my existence through His light and love.

With a positive state of mind, I realized that I could communicate directly with God and learn directly from Him. My thoughts, first communicated to God, were to know more of Him. I wanted to know more about Him who had now become known to me as my God and Creator. I wanted to know more about Him than anything else in His creation. He conveyed that my search to know Him would take an eternity, and that He would always be there for me to call upon to learn more about Him and from Him.

I wanted to know more about my origin as a spiritual being. God revealed to me that I had been created as a spiritual being at the beginning of the creation of the universe to inhabit the universe on a spiritual level and to exist in spiritual schools of learning in preparation for further growth and understanding. Part of this experience for myself and for all other spiritual beings is the necessity to be born into a physical body and to become part of the human experience. It was God's plan to enable the spiritual beings of the universe to grow in His image and likeness through the spiritual journey in the universe, but it was also part of God's plan to create a physical world as a place of learning and growth.

God gave each of us an intellect, memory, and free will to enter upon our learning experience in the universe. Part of our mission as spiritual beings included taking form as humans and learning from our journey in the physical world before returning to the spiritual world through the process we know as death.

As spiritual beings, we began our journey in the universe following our creation by gravitating to soul groups for purposes of learning and growing in our spiritual state in preparation for our incarnation in the physical world as humans. We gravitated toward particular groups because we individually and collectively had like interests and missions to accomplish during our spiritual journey. We remained as spirits in these soul groups to grow and learn in a spiritual state until the progress of the material part of the universe created conditions appropriate for us to begin that part of our journey that allowed us to incarnate and experience the "human condition."

God revealed the destination of our spiritual journey to me. It is our goal, individually and collectively, through all history and time, and through all dimensions and space, to reunite and become one with God. Only at that point will we individually or collectively realize our total mission and purpose for existence in God's eyes. The attainment of our goals and purpose in this life can be achieved by our coming into attunement with God's plan for us. It is a simple path that leads to our self-discovery of what God's plan is for us: Love of God! Love of self! Love of others! Service to our fellow man and community.

CHAPTER 6

THE AMPHITHEATER

Dan was back at my side again. We descended together from God's light into a universe of bright stars. We were again in the deepest void of space, but now I felt comfortable in this environment as well as in my spirit body, and I felt at home in this celestial location.

As Dan and I continued to descend, I was startled by the magnificent ethereal structure directly below us. The heavenly structure resembled an amphitheater similar to those found in ancient civilizations. This amphitheater was made of a brilliant, crystal-like substance that radiated multi-colored waves of energy throughout its form. The amphitheater was suspended in the void of space in the same fashion that a space station might hover in space. The amphitheater was similar in size to a sports stadium and conveyed a great majesty.

As Dan and I descended closer to the amphitheater, I realized that it was filled with thousands of spiritual beings. We hovered directly over the structure, and I felt a vibrant energy envelop me. The energy seemed to come from the crystalline structure of the amphitheater.

The lower we descended, the more I was drawn to the energy.

I sensed that the thousands of spiritual beings there were also absorbing this energy. They were sending out waves of energy to one another as well as to Dan and me. We were now descending onto the celestial field, which was surrounded by the large arc of the amphitheater. Although I first felt it as energy, I recognized that the energy emanating from the crystalline structure was also a symphonic sound.

Soon Dan and I were suspended in the center of the celestial field which meant that we were the focus of attention for the thousands of spiritual beings positioned throughout the amphitheater. Above, below, and behind us was the deep void of space. In front of us, thousands of spiritual beings were communicating, by musical sounds, feelings of goodwill to me. Their sounds of greeting were in harmony with the symphonic sounds of energy emanating from the amphitheater. Once I settled onto the celestial field, I could look directly into the crystalline surface of the amphitheater and watch as multi-colored prisms of light pulsated through the structure.

I was overwhelmed by the awesome sight before me, but the feelings of love that were conveyed to me by the spiritual beings were even more overwhelming. The spiritual beings were cheering me, conveying loving encouragement and support. "You are doing wonderfully. We are here to support you. Continue to do good work, and we will help you. You are part of us, and we are part of you. We stand ready to come to your aid when you need us, and you will. Call us. Beckon us. We will flock to you when the time comes!"

Frankly, I was confused by all the attention. There wasn't anything wonderful about the way I had conducted my life. Perhaps the spiritual beings were speaking of what was yet to come. They certainly could not have been speaking of earlier events in my life.

I thought, *How can I be doing wonderfully? I almost killed someone tonight. Could I be justified in what I tried to do?*

Dan interceded. "You were spiritually rescued from a negative event that was taking place in your life. You just tried to communicate a negative thought concerning this event. You cannot speak of such things here. There are no negative thoughts here, only positive affirmations. They cannot hear you; they will not hear you when you speak or think in negativity. You must be positive to perform your mission."

I turned to my right, realizing that a group of spiritual beings had joined us on the celestial field. This event was indeed a homecoming for me. Among the group of spiritual beings, I recognized deceased friends and relatives from my life. I also recognized other friends from my spiritual life prior to my birth on earth. I was filled with joy when I recognized my grandparents, aunts, and uncles who had died during my life. However, I was disappointed because I did not see my dad among the group. I then recognized other friends from my life, including a girl from high school. I did not know she had died. The feelings of love and joy that I shared with these relatives and friends were far beyond the emotions I had shared with them during my life. As the child of an alcoholic and broken home, I did not communicate feelings to relatives or friends very well. In fact, I wasn't aware that I had many feelings. Most of my feelings were hidden inside.

Now that I was at my homecoming as a spiritual being, the greetings were the kind that I had imagined took place in a healthy family. It seemed as if we were

celebrating every major holiday, every birth and birthday, every wonderful event in all of our lives in a
manner that we could never celebrate as mortal human
beings. I wanted this celebration and homecoming to
continue forever, but a silence suddenly fell across the
crowded amphitheater.

All attention seemed to be directed to the celestial
field around me, and a shimmering, luminescent sphere
enveloped me, making me feel as if I had stepped into a
crystal globe. Although I was aware that the crystalline
sphere was suspended on the celestial field in view of all
the spiritual beings in attendance, I found myself in a
different celestial realm. Somehow the spiritual beings
were still observing me inside this crystal sphere. I realized why the hush of silence had fallen over the crowd:
My life review was about to begin—in public, it seemed.

CHAPTER 7

MY LIFE REVIEW

I'm gonna be like you, Dad!
You know I'm gonna be like you!
(Harry Chapin, "Cat's in the Cradle")

The visual reality of the crystalline sphere was different from any concept of reality that I had ever experienced. I was enveloped in a realm of consciousness devoid of time or space. As I acclimated myself to this environment, I was given an orientation on how the process would proceed.

I was aware that I was about to review every event, thought, emotion, and experience of my life. I became aware that the purpose of the review was for me to evaluate my life in terms of my intended mission as a human, to review my life in a manner that permitted me to focus on the areas that provided the most important experiences in terms of my spiritual growth and development.

Although I was alone in the crystalline sphere, I was aware that I was in the presence of God and watched over by the many spiritual beings in the amphitheater who were encouraging me with their love and support. Nothing about my life was a secret to God, nor to the spiritual beings, yet I did not perceive that I was being judged. I realized that all who were part of God's spiritual creation had fallen from God and had made mistakes in their own journeys. There was no one among the assemblage of spiritual beings who was about to cast the first stone at me.

I was going to need support to give me the courage and strength to review my life. Before proceeding with surgery on a physical body, an anesthesiologist administers drugs to block out the pain. In the spiritual world, the opposite effect is desired during the life review. I was provided with the spiritual strength to soberly review my life for the first time ever without my "blocking it out" to avoid the reality of what I had experienced.

I realized it was I who would be conducting the review. What had I done with my life? Where was my life going? What had I done to show love of God, love of my neighbor, love of self? What had I done to be of service to mankind? These were the important questions I would have to consider.

Since the crystalline sphere was not encumbered by the limiting properties of time and space, I was going to reexperience my life with the same intensity with which it was originally experienced. I would be in control of the review and have the ability to slow the process and concentrate on the lessons to be learned during significant experiences.

Suddenly, the surface of the crystalline sphere dissolved from its translucent state into a grayish opaque surface. My life review began as the surface of the sphere came alive with a vivid and lifelike scene that took me back to my infancy. The scene was not just lifelike; it was reality itself. I was a third-person witness to events that I had not previously witnessed.

My life review began with a scene on the evening of March 21, 1947, in a boisterous, overcrowded, and smoky high school gymnasium in Williamsport, Pennsylvania. I recognized my young father. He was pacing up and down the sidelines, coaching his team. His face was beet-red, and his neck and facial muscles bulged as he screamed out his orders.

My dad was a local hero. He had returned from World War II to coach the St. Gabriel's High School basketball team to an undefeated regular season. Dad's G-Men became the first team in the history of the Anthracite League to win the championship without losing a single game. Now Dad's team was playing the much larger Pittsburgh Central Catholic High School for the Catholic State Championship. It was the biggest night of Dad's basketball career. This game had been promoted as David versus Goliath: the little school from Hazleton's Donegal Hill against the larger and more powerful team from Pittsburgh. Yet Dad's smaller team came out in their purple and white uniforms and led through the whole game. The hard-fought first period ended in a 6–6 tie, but the G-Men stepped up the pace in the second quarter to grab an 18–14 lead at half-time. The third period gave no indication of the trouble to come as St. Gabriel's boosted their margin to 24–18.

Pittsburgh came back strong to cut the margin to 30–29 with two minutes left, and set the stage for a Pittsburgh player to throw the winning toss, a mid-court set shot, as Pittsburgh went up 31–30. But time had not run out, and the G-Men moved the ball down the court. A corner jump shot at the buzzer seemed to sink through the net, but at the last moment it caught the rim, rolled around, and up, and out, as the buzzer sounded.

I was suddenly standing in Mom and Dad's bedroom on that same night watching my little six-month-old self sleeping comfortably, secure in my crib, blissfully unaware that my dad had just suffered the pain of defeat. As I viewed myself as a sleeping infant, I had no idea that a missed shot in a high school basketball game could have such a significant effect on the rest of *my* life. That was the night my dad's drinking went out of control. He never stopped drinking until I buried him in the summer of 1974. He died broken and lonely at 57 years old.

My life review fast-forwarded to the night of Dad's funeral. I sat in a Hazleton bar with some of my relatives and a few of Dad's old friends. The old-timers began to relive that game, the first and only game Dad lost that season. Although he coached the same team of veteran players the following year, his drinking had started to interfere with his coaching (or vice versa), and that next season was not a winning one.

As the old-timers finished reliving that championship game play by play, one of my dad's friends pulled me aside. "You know, son, your dad was a good man. Every one of us admired and respected him, but I watched him the night of the championship game when the final shot rolled around the rim and fell out. Your dad clutched his head and doubled over. His face got redder and redder. When he stood back up, he looked like he wasn't even there. He had a vacant stare in his eyes that I will never forget, you know, that thousand-mile stare. He once told me that he felt like someone had poured acid on his brain when he lost that game; it hurt him so deeply. I don't think he could ever stop drinking after that because it was the only thing that would dull the pain. Funny thing is he would never talk about that game, but I knew it was always on his mind."

As this scene ended, I recalled how I had frequently pulled out Dad's old basketball album and relived that championship season as well as that fateful game. I always envisioned myself standing invisibly next to my dad watching his every coaching move. I even tried to think my way into his head and examine his brain as if I could somehow find and heal the defect and retroactively change everything. I always wanted to know what that pain was like for Dad. It was also most painful for me because it would come to distance him from me. Years later, I would learn to experience that pain myself.

As my life review continued, I saw myself going to St. Gabriel's cemetery on Memorial Day when I was five years old. It was a tradition for the veterans of World Wars I and II and the Korean War to gather first at Crossin's Tavern before convening at the cemetery. As the veterans gathered in a circle to prepare for the twenty-one-gun salute, I looked up at Dad and his friends. The men were dressed in suits and ties along with their veterans' hats and sashes. They were all red-faced and laughing heartily. I watched as they passed a gleaming silver flask from man to man. The flask sparkled in the sunlight and blinded me briefly as Dad took a long drink and passed it on. It seemed to me that in the world of men this ritual with the flask was as important as the ritual of the chalice in the church. They marched to the ceremony area with a lone bugler who played "Taps." As the men raised their rifles and shot each of the rounds, we small kids dove to the grass to retrieve the spent shells.

After leaving the cemetery, we walked to Crossin's Tavern to celebrate the rest of the holiday. I looked up into the crowd of men around me at the bar, watching all those war heroes, those veterans, and wanting to be just like them. At one point, Dad picked me up in his arms and placed me on the barstool. This, by the way, was an Irish neighborhood bar; a family gathering place. I watched as he passed a glass of beer to my lips, and I sipped it. It tasted bitter, and I didn't like it, but I swallowed it anyway because I wanted to be just like Dad and his friends. All of the men reached out with their beer glasses in my direction and saluted me. It was a ritual of passage for sons to have their first beer with their dads, and this was my time.

"Hear! Hear!" they cheered. "Now, he's a real man!" At five years old, I felt like I was.

My life review continued. Not long after that first beer, things got bad at home. When I was a little kid, I guess I didn't realize that things were going badly between Mom and Dad, at least not at first. Maybe things had already been bad, but I was too young to notice. Dad started coming home later at night. At first, I would wait for him. Later, I would hide from him. Sometimes I would lie on the couch with Mom and wait. As we heard him come up the steps to the apartment, Mom would begin to shiver. The louder his footsteps, the worse he was going to be, and the more she would shiver. Most nights we were lucky. He would come through the door and bounce down the hallway hitting the walls until he found the bedroom and passed out. Those were the good nights.

The worst of the bad nights, and the last of them, was the night he pulled Mom from the couch and threatened to throw her down the stairs. I got in between them and began to scream and hit him. I tried to make myself bigger, trying to hop out of my skin, so that somehow I would be big enough to stop him. But I couldn't, and I found myself at the bottom of the stairs with Mom who was badly bruised. I was so proud of her when she got up from the floor, and we both walked out of the apartment. It was the last time for her, but, of course, he was my dad. I would search for him and seek him out for years to come.

Mom and I moved to my grandmother's house that night, and was I ever glad. My only sibling—my sister, Kay, who was two years older—was already living there. Gram's house was big, spacious, and peaceful. I even had my own room. The best part was the yard surrounded by privet hedges. A single umbrella tree filled the yard with shade. Gram had a sofa swing under the tree, and I would spend my youthful summers swinging back and forth on that swing, reading books mostly, and waiting for something to happen.

Grandpa had passed away the year before we moved there. Gram was running Grandpa's general store in a nearby coal town, Stockton, where she was also the post-mistress. Gram finally decided to close the store because Stockton had become a dying town. The following summer, Mom and I moved to East Hampton, New York, where my mother became a summer camp counselor, and I became one of the campers. At the end of the summer, Mom stayed in New York to work, and I came back to Hazleton to live with Gram and my sister. I watched *Father Knows Best* and *Ozzie and Harriet* on Gram's black and white TV. I adopted these TV families as my own to give me a sense of how things were supposed to be.

Gram had told me that Dad was just sick, but he would get better. When he got better, Mom would come back from New York, and we would be a family again. Gram had told me this story while I was helping her prune her rose bushes in the garden. When Gram told me that things were going to get better, I purposely pricked my finger on a rose thorn and drew blood. Somehow I knew she was wrong; Dad and Mom were not going to get back together again.

Gram's house was on Elm Street, three blocks east and up Donegal Hill from St. Gabriel's parish. The parish church was a magnificent structure with a gothic stone facade and two majestic spires that surrounded a large circular stained glass window. The parish also included an imposing rectory, a Sisters of Mercy convent, and a grade school and high school. The parish was the center of activity for the residents of Donegal Hill, vying particularly for the men's time with the Irish bars that dotted the neighborhood.

It was an easy walk to church and school from Gram's house, and there were many kids in the neighborhood. According to Gram, I was the man of the house, especially after my sister moved to New York to live with my mother. Being the only kid on the block who was the man of the house made me special.

Our Catholicism was an integral part of our lives at that time. I was growing up in a Catholic school, going to Mass, confession, and communion. During Lent, Gram and I would say the rosary every night. Religion was spoon-fed, and we didn't question what we were taught; we just accepted it. Every year we would have religious retreat weeks. This meant that visiting priests would come to the church and school and terrorize us into a more focused attention to our religious obligations. I remembered that these retreats were also very enlightening.

As my life review continued, I relived one particular retreat sermon that I had heard when I was eleven years old. The priest pointed and shook his finger at us as he said in a very threatening voice, "Any man who spills his seed on the ground will burn in hell for all eternity!"

I walked out of the church feeling numb and dizzy, walking the three blocks to Gram's house as if it was a death march. I kept thinking about all the times that I had peed in Gram's bushes instead of going inside to the bathroom. I went on to spend the better part of the next year living a fearful existence, in dread that I was going to burn in hell for all eternity for peeing on the ground. Quite convinced that my soul was beyond salvation, I had morbid thoughts and nightmares that my destiny was already determined to be in the flaming holocaust. In retrospect, I had become so absorbed with the finality of the afterlife as a place of suffering and pain that I began to equivocate between a belief in a burning, eternal afterlife and a concept that all life mercifully ended upon death.

Shortly after that dreaded sermon, I was walking along Elm Street to Gram's house while morbidly deep in thought about whether or not I was going to burn in hell for all eternity or simply cease to exist upon death. I had worked myself into a considerable depression over this predicament. As I walked along feeling worse and worse about my state of existence, I suddenly sensed a bright beam of golden light before me. As I tried to focus my eyes, which were temporarily blinded by the light, I thought I saw an angel in the light, and then I heard a powerful voice say to me, "Do not be afraid! . . . Everything will be okay!"

As the message echoed in my ears, the light disappeared, and I found myself standing alone on the quiet street. I turned and walked into Gram's house. I went upstairs to my bedroom and lay on my bed. I began to question in my mind whether or not I had just seen an angel. I was not sure, but I was certain that something had come over me like a protective mantle. As a result, I no longer had that fear of burning in hell because I had peed in the bushes. Several years later, I discovered what the "seed" was all about. That was the same time I started losing my interest in religion and taking up an interest in girls.

As I reviewed this part of my life, I saw that it was the first time I believed that I finally deserved all the repressed guilt that I had been carrying around for most of my young life. As Catholics, we were instructed to feel guilty, even though we didn't understand why we should. A new girl had moved into the neighborhood for the summer, and I wanted her. She was my first dysfunctional relationship. I wanted to impress her by taking her to the candy store. Since Gram was not home and I needed some money, I took five dollars from her purse. It was the first time I tried to use money to impress a girl. It was the beginning of a pattern of behavior that I would continue into my adult years, using money and material possessions to attract and control women.

My life review continued. During the years I lived with Gram, Dad was living in a boarding house somewhere near Wyoming Street, just north of St. Gabriel's parish. I had no communication with him, but I saw him frequently sitting inside the window of a tavern on Wyoming Street. Almost every day during lunch hour, my friends and I would walk to Moye's candy store and back to school, passing the tavern window. Usually my dad would be sitting there. He always seemed to be distant from me. Certainly, he knew who I was, but he seemed not to recognize me. He always sat at the end of the bar with his back to the street-front window. Occasionally, I would see him turn and stare out the window, especially when someone opened the door and walked into the tavern. It seemed like he was always waiting for someone to walk through the door to make his life right for him.

I once followed Dad at night to his rooming house in an alleyway off Wyoming Street to see where he lived. I watched from the alleyway as he stumbled up the stairway and into his room. The next day I waited for him to go to the tavern. As I watched him climb onto his barstool, I ran down the alleyway and up the stairway of the boarding house and opened the unlocked door to the room he had entered the night before. It was a dark, dingy room with a single window. My heart was pounding, and I began to sweat profusely. I could see out the cloudy window and down into the tavern window where Dad was still sitting at the bar. I looked through the old chest of drawers. They contained his clothes, except for the night table drawer, which held some coins, and keys and things, but not what I was looking for. Whenever we had to write cards at school, like Christmas or Valentine's Day cards, I would send cards to Dad. I would address the envelopes to the tavern on Wyoming Street. I was hoping I would find those cards in his room, but I didn't. I wanted to know that somehow Dad considered me a part of his life. When I didn't find any cards I ran down the stairs, out into the alleyway, and all the way back to Gram's. I ran upstairs to my room and collapsed on my bed, out of breath. I had a gnawing pain in my gut, and it would not go away. That pain stayed with me for many years after.

During the summer before my first year of high school, I practiced basketball every day. I thought that my dad would have to notice me if I was good at basketball. Outside of his drinking, I thought that basketball was the only other thing that was important in his life. By the night of the first game, I was good enough to be one of the first reserve players. When I was finally called into the game, I felt confident. I remember dribbling the ball down the court toward the crowd when I looked up and saw my dad weaving drunkenly down the aisle. He was trying to yell something encouraging to me, I thought, but I was momentarily stunned, and I dribbled the ball off my foot and out of bounds. I looked foolish and felt worse. I saw my dad waving his arm in my direction in disgust. That was our only communication for years. I stood frozen on the spot staring at a crack in the hardwood floor, and I wanted to crawl into it. Shortly after that, I quit playing basketball.

After graduating from high school, I moved to New York City to live with my mother and her new husband, Michael, who became like a father to me. Gram and I had become best buddies in our home on Elm Street, and it broke my heart to leave her and our home in Hazleton. I always wanted to take care of Gram to show my appreciation. Gram would have been left alone in the big house on Elm Street, so she moved to New York to live with my mother's sister. Gram was saddened when she had to give up her home. She had a sharp wit well into her seventies, but in her eighties she developed hardening of the arteries. She no longer recognized me and died several years later in a nursing home in Queens, New York.

I was reluctant to leave Hazleton because I thought that if I left I would never see my dad again. There was no other reason to go back to Hazleton. All my high school friends had gone on to college or joined the military, and I had enrolled at St. John's University in Queens. It was at St. John's in my freshman year that I learned how to reconnect with my dad. All through high school, I couldn't stand the stench of beer or the odor of alcohol. It reminded me of how my dad's drinking had ruined my family life. Whenever my high school friends got together and we tried to drink, we would usually turn green and throw up. But St. John's was a party school, and the fraternity system was the epitome of the social scene. I was invited to a party at Phi Kappa Tau, the best fraternity on campus. What I remember of that party was that I chugged a lot of beer, and I threw up a lot, but so did the other freshmen. I just kept chugging beer and enjoying the party. I felt a new bond with this fraternity of men who knew how to party. Drinking was fun. The atmosphere at the party reminded me of the time I was five years old, watching my dad and his friends in Crossin's Tavern.

When I crawled out of bed the next morning and into the bathroom, I looked at myself in the mirror. I looked pale and sickly; my skin was chalk white. The whites of my eyes were bloodshot and yellow, but I felt great inside. Sure, I was as sick as a dog, but something had happened the night before, amidst all the camaraderie, that made me feel good inside. I felt a sense of belonging that was new for me. Most of all, the gnawing feeling in my gut that I had had since I was a little kid had disappeared while I was drinking. Maybe it was only for a fleeting moment, but the drinking made me feel better. I believed that it was the medicine I needed to deal with the pain. As I looked into the bathroom mirror into those baggy eyes and that pale and sickly face, I confidently said to myself, "Hear! Hear! Now I'm a real man!"

My life review continued. My initiation into drinking and enjoying beer gave me a new sense of courage. It was time for me to visit my dad. I took a bus from New York City to Hazleton to visit him. Of course, I knew just where to find him. I walked from the bus station to his tavern. He was still sitting on his favorite bar stool just inside the window. As I opened the door and walked in, he turned and looked, just as I had seen him do so many times before. There was a glimmer of recognition in his eyes as I pulled myself up onto a barstool next to him.

The bartender, a ruddy, older Irishman, dressed in a white shirt and apron with a black tie, placed a coaster in front of me. "What'll it be?" he said.

"A draft beer for me and one for my dad here!" The sound of my voice saying "dad" seemed to unsettle him, as if he were embarrassed by the reality of his father-hood. He looked pensively toward me, and I saw a soft-ness in his face that I had never seen before. He seemed somewhat at peace with himself.

"How are you doing, Son. . . . It sure is good to see you." When I heard him say it was good to see me, that was important to me. He motioned to the glass when I put it back on the bar after a long, thirst-quenching quaff. "When did you start drinking beer?"

"Oh, not long ago. I just have a couple of beers now and then, no big deal," I bragged.

He laughed to himself, a cynical laugh, and then he turned further toward me. He seemed to speak with a wisdom that was beyond my comprehension. "No big deal, you say. Well, let's hope not. Just make sure you keep it to a couple of beers, now and then."

Dad and I spent the rest of the afternoon at the tavern. We now had a connection to each other, some-thing that we could share together, a glass of beer. I felt a bond with my dad develop through the afternoon. Before that day, I had never had the courage to approach my dad, man to man, to look him in the eye, to talk to him. The glass of beer gave me the courage to do that. Everything changed for me that afternoon. I now had that one connection with my dad, part of a relationship that I had longed for. It would last for ten more years during my infrequent trips to Hazleton, until he died.

We talked slowly at first that afternoon. There were long pauses in our conversation, especially when the door opened behind us. Dad would always turn to see who was coming through the door, sometimes greeting a new patron. Then he would turn back to the bar and take a long draw on his glass, usually emptying it and pushing it toward the bartender. I had my money on the bar, and I would push it across the bar. I was buying the beers that day for my dad, and I was proud of it. Sometimes the bartender would take my money; sometimes he would just smile, knock on the bar, and say, "Not this time, sonny. This one's on the house!"

As the afternoon drew on, I noticed that Dad would hold his glass in his burly hand while he twisted it slowly counterclockwise in a continuous motion. He would sometimes turn the glass backwards more quickly when he seemed to be deep in thought. Sometimes he would stare down into his glass of beer and stop turning it. Then he would chug the rest of the beer and push the glass across the bar for a refill.

As the afternoon turned to evening, my courage grew, as did my desire to know my dad. Pointing to his glass as he turned it, I finally asked him, "Why do you do that?"

"Why do I do what?" he asked, staring at his glass.

"Why do you turn your glass like that? You've been doing it all day. I kind of wondered if you realized that . . . that you keep twisting your glass around in your hand."

Dad stared down at his glass, and the glass stopped turning. There was another long pause in our conversation as I looked closely at my dad's sad eyes. He seemed resigned to his fate in life. I flashed back to my early childhood, remembering how his energy would burst out in anger and rage when he was drinking. Now it seemed as if he had run out of energy; he seemed to be tired of his life. Dad looked down the length of the bar with a faraway expression, as if he were looking into another time and place. The glass started turning backwards again, and he told me his story.

"Son, you were too young to remember what happened to your mother and me. When you were just a little kid, I used to come home too many times having had too many beers. I wasn't very nice to your mother then. I guess one night I just had one too many. I don't remember much of what I did, but when it was over, your mother was lying on the bottom of the stairs. You were there, too, both of you screaming at me. Your mother took you away that night, and it's been hard for me to face you ever since then."

He drew a long sip of beer and continued. "After it was all over, I found myself alone in that apartment, knowing I had done something terribly wrong. I went down to the street, but you and your mother were gone, so I went back to the bar and started drinking again to calm my nerves. As I looked down into the glass each time it was emptied, I turned the glass backwards, while trying to think back to what had just happened. I turned the glass backwards like the minute hand on a clock. I guess I thought that if I turned it backwards enough times, I could remember what happened and somehow make it not happen. I knew that your mother was gone from me for good that night, but as sorry as I was, I couldn't turn back that clock, and I couldn't change what happened that night."

Dad took a long gulp from his glass and put it back down on the bar. It seemed as if his eyes were filling with tears as he continued to stare down the bar, the glass still turning counterclockwise in his hand.

As the years went by until Dad died, I went to Hazleton as often as I could, maybe four or five times a year. Most of my friends there were gone. They had either graduated from college and moved away, or they were in the military. Hazleton was for many of us a forgotten town, someplace you came from but didn't go back to. Dad had moved into his own small apartment by then, and he had a telephone, but he was never home when I called. I would send him cards at Christmas and on his birthday, and sometimes I would send gifts.

By New Year's Eve, 1973, I thought I was pretty successful. I had opened my own real estate office in the Hamptons, and I had a pretty girlfriend named Ginnie. She had lost her father when she was young, so she had an affinity for my dad. While we were getting ready to go out for New Year's Eve, Ginnie said, "Let's not go to this boring party. Let's drive up to Hazleton and visit your dad tonight."

She knew that I had been thinking of him all that day. As crazy as it seemed, I agreed that it was a good idea, so we drove up to Hazleton and walked into Dad's bar just before midnight. He was at his corner seat as usual, and his eyes lit up when he saw us walk through the door. Dad loved Ginnie, and we had a great time that night with Dad and his tavern friends, dancing in the narrow aisle to the jukebox and singing all night long. It was the first and only time since I was five years old that I remembered having a fun time with my dad.

On New Year's Day, we took Dad to breakfast. He sat across from us, and for the first time in his life, I saw some happiness, almost contentment, in his smile. I could tell he was happy for me, and that now, somewhere in his sad and lonely life, there was some fulfillment. He had a relationship with his son, and I knew that it meant something to him. Dad didn't eat his breakfast, and I realized that I had never seen him eat food. This was the first time we had ever sat in a restaurant together; in the past, we had always met in his favorite bar. Ten years had gone by since I first sat down next to Dad in his bar. I realized that the years of hard drinking were finally taking their toll on Dad's health. His complexion was almost chalk white, except for his nose which was swollen and red with broken veins. He moved slowly, breathing deeply and wheezing heavily.

It was during the month of June 1974 when I got the call. Dad had been admitted to St. Joseph's Hospital in Hazleton and transferred quickly to a hospital in Scranton. The doctor suggested that I come to Scranton to meet with him. That afternoon I was sitting before the doctor in Scranton as he described Dad's condition. He had advanced cirrhosis of the liver. The doctor had already given me the prognosis, but I continued to ask questions, choosing not to hear what he had said. Dad was going to get better; it was just that simple; nothing else would be acceptable.

When I walked into Dad's room, I realized that I had already lost him. He was angry and upset, and he glared at me. It was Dad as I remembered him from when I was a little boy. He thrashed about on the bed, flailing his weakened arms. Dementia had already set in.

I walked out of the hospital and across the street to a tavern. It was the kind of place that my dad would have liked. As I sat alone drinking, I thought about what had happened to Dad, and I analyzed his life of drinking. He had allowed his drinking to get out of control. His drinking controlled him, and now it was killing him. The difference between my dad and me was that my drinking was controlled. I actually thought that I was much smarter than he was, and that I was too smart to allow my drinking to affect my life. I was successful in every respect: I had a nice car, new home, and my own business. I wanted my dad to know that I was successful. I wanted my dad to be proud of his son, and

I knew that he was, but I knew how to control my drinking, and Dad did not, and that was the difference between us. Or so I thought. . . .

After we buried Dad in St. Gabriel's Cemetery, Ginnie and I decided to get away for awhile. Instead of turning east on Interstate 80 and going back to New York, we decided to drive west without a plan. Several days later, I was driving across Nebraska and thinking about my life with Dad. Ginnie was taking a nap as we traveled west on Interstate 80 crossing the rolling plains. I was listening to a new song on the radio, "Cat's in the Cradle," by Harry Chapin. When I listened to the words, I heard a story similar to the story of my life with Dad: "I'm gonna be like you, Dad! . . . You know I'm gonna be like you!"

For the first time in my young adult life, I began to cry. As each chorus and verse filled the air, the song became increasingly personal to me.

"When you coming home, Son? . . . I don't know when. . . . But we'll get together then, Dad. . . . You know we'll have a good time then! . . . We're gonna have a good time then!"

I thought about all the opportunities to visit Dad more often that I had missed, but now those opportunities were gone. As I drove across the Nebraska plains, emotions welled up inside me that I had buried for years. Those buried emotions came out as a river of tears.

As the song played on, I thought about how many times I had mentally tried to change things back to what they might have been, to that last championship game. Like my dad, who twirled his glass counterclockwise to undo his fate, I was a dreamer. Yet no matter how much I dreamed, I couldn't change anything that had happened in Dad's life, a life that went out of control. As the song ended, a chill went up and down my spine. I sat frozen in my seat, while the car seemed to take on a life of its own as it drove down the deserted highway. I was riveted to the view in my rearview mirror. I was looking at the ghost of my dad sitting in the back seat. His large frame, bloated by years of drinking, filled the mirror. He was staring straight at me with those sad eyes, his face swollen and sagging, aged and defeated.

The last lines of the song were suspended in time and space, and I heard the last verse of the song, not from Harry Chapin's melodious voice, but from the deep, gruff, and graveled voice of my dad: "He's grown up just like me! . . . My boy, he's just like me!"

I sat staring into the rearview mirror for an eternal moment, watching the ghost of my dad in the back seat. Certainly this is a hallucination, I thought. My dad was dead and gone forever. But I was comforted by the experience.

Perhaps a spirit of my dad still existed, and perhaps somehow he was communicating with me. I continued to stare at the mirror, transfixed and motionless, sharing that moment with him, somehow thinking that it would be the last, and then he was gone.

CHAPTER 8

LIFE OUT OF SYNC

Koyaanisqatsi: Crazy life, life in turmoil, life disintegrating, life out of balance, a state of life that
calls for another way of living!

—*Hopi Indian word*

I was still enveloped in a visual realm of consciousness as my life review traveled through my past.

When my dad died, I was left alone with the only
bond that remained between us. I had "inherited" his
alcoholism. I knew I was an alcoholic. I acknowledged
it. I accepted it. I had started drinking in 1964, and I
buried my dad in 1974 when my own drinking career
was ten years old.

I didn't have a problem with inheriting my father's
disease. Actually, I welcomed it. I enjoyed drinking. It was
my best friend. Besides, there was no reason why I could
not continue to drink. I looked at my drinking as a gift,
not as a curse. Although I readily accepted that I was an
alcoholic like my dad, my alcoholism was something that

I had under control. Drinking was the bond that would keep Dad's memory with me forever. Since I was willing to acknowledge my alcoholism, I assumed that I was mature and responsible enough to drink. Because I knew I was an alcoholic, I would know how to handle it. The difference between Dad and me was that I could control my drinking. It was not going to ruin my life as it had ruined my dad's life. I believed I would continue to drink throughout my adult life without any repercussions. Drinking would always be a part of my life. I couldn't live without it.

Following my dad's death, my life fell into a comfortable routine. My real estate business was flourishing; in fact, the business began to run itself. For several years, I had been spending more and more of my time at a pub down the street from my office. I would go there for lunch and sometimes remain there all afternoon. I had my own reserved stool at the corner of the bar from where I had a view of the street. Each time the front door opened, I would automatically look to see who was coming through the door. The telephone was located next to my corner of the bar, so I could stay in contact with the office. The truth is that I was more comfortable at that bar than in my own home. I felt like that pub room was my own living room. From my corner of the bar, I could run my real estate business by telephone. I was totally in control.

I would awaken every morning with a gnawing feeling in my stomach, a feeling that would always make me want to get out of bed and out of the house. Since the gnawing feeling reminded me of my dad, it drove me to be successful. I was driven out of fear of failure. I didn't want to turn out like my dad. By noon, the gnawing feeling would shift to acceptable hunger pains, so I would go to the pub for lunch. As soon as I began to drink, the gnawing feeling would begin to ease up.

I soon became bored with my real estate business and decided I was more interested in the bar business, denying to myself that I was really more interested in spending all my time in a bar.

As my life review continued, I watched myself sitting in the pub from a different perspective. I recognized that I had wasted most of my precious time sitting at a bar, but I somehow justified it. I was studying the bar business from a patron's perspective. I had never worked in a bar or restaurant, but I certainly became an expert as a patron. I began to frequent as many different bars and clubs as I could. I wanted to learn the business from the other side of the bar. I always had an excuse for being in a bar.

By 1975, times were changing rapidly for the Baby Boomer generation. Nixon had resigned. The Vietnam War was over. The Baby Boomers discarded their bell-bottoms and protest signs. The nation began to emerge from a long recession. College graduates were flocking en masse to New York City to pursue business careers, and they converged by the thousands on the Hamptons for summer weekends. The bars and clubs were jammed with young people who were trying to forget Vietnam by partying into the future. I was among them, observing while drinking and dreaming, waiting for my opportunity to get into the bar business.

My opportunity came in the spring of 1976. The largest building on the same street as my real estate office had a huge airplane hangar-type space that was being under-utilized as a warehouse. I had dreamed about this building for several years as the ideal location for a nightclub, and it was finally put up for sale. Suddenly, I knew my dream was about to come true. I was going to create the greatest nightclub in the Hamptons.

The owner of the building requested that I do an appraisal of the building, so I was given access to the spacious warehouse and left alone. I began to take measurements of the wide-open space with its twenty-foot-high ceilings when something very unusual happened. I sat against the wall of the warehouse, when suddenly it seemed as if I was in a nightclub filled with people. The lights, the sounds, and the excitement were almost vividly real. It seemed more real than a dream.

I began to sketch the layout of the club. I did not have any design or architectural training or experience, nor did I have any experience in the bar, restaurant, or nightclub business. As I first looked out over the open space before me, I envisioned a dance floor surrounded by an elevated amphitheater of seating tiers where patrons would sit at tables while observing the dance floor. Along the longest wall directly opposite the tiers and dance floor, I visualized the largest bar in the Hamptons. In a matter of minutes, I had sketched out the entire layout of the club, just as I had envisioned it, and just as it was to be built for its opening only three months later.

As I walked out the front door of the building I crossed Main Street, sat on a park bench, and began to sketch the front of the building. A creative flow of energy, one that I had not previously experienced, was responsible for the inspiration that allowed me to quickly design the interior of the club. I felt the same process from a different perspective, as I concentrated on the front facade of the building, which inspired ideas for the name and the theme of the club.

Since the front of the building was white stucco and appeared to be a design more appropriate for a tropical or desert environment, I began to have vivid visions of exotic and faraway places. I envisioned India and the Sudan during the British colonial period, and the names "Bombay" and "Khartoum" came to me. I envisioned doormen at the entrance to the club in British military uniforms from the 1800s. Then my vision moved to French-colonial Morocco, to Casablanca and Marrakech.

Casablanca had always been my favorite movie. I empathized with the role of Rick, played by Humphrey Bogart. The nightclub owner wins the woman in distress. They fall in love, surrounded by danger and intrigue. Then he loses the love of his life, and finds himself alone, melancholic, reflecting over the intensity of the romance, the fleeting moment in time. He returns to more comfortable surroundings, sitting in his bar with his best friend, the bottle, drinking and thinking and dreaming.

The more I daydreamed about the theme, the more I leaned toward a Moroccan theme. Marrakech was romantic, mysterious, and intriguing. It was a desert city on the edge of the Sahara and a trade outpost for smuggling guns and drugs. How appropriate. The name of the place would be Marrakech with a slightly different spelling: Club Marakesh.

The visions of exotic places that I had were like déjà vu experiences, as were the visions I had that resulted in my design of the club. I could already envision the look of the place, the reaction of the crowds as they entered, the sounds and lights filling the vast space, and the intensity of the energy level. These were all new sensations for me as if I had tapped into inner resources of which I was not previously aware.

From that day on, events proceeded rapidly as the summer season quickly approached. Ginnie was working in my real estate business, and I formed a business partnership with her and several others. Although I preferred being independent in business, I needed other investors. Under the new arrangement, I assumed that I would be able to remain in control of the venture.

My life review continued, as I watched myself jumping into the construction phase enthusiastically, interviewing and engaging carpenters, electricians, plumbers, painters, and other contractors to build the club. As I took each of the prospective trade workers through the empty warehouse explaining their assignments, they looked around the space and listened to my timetable for completion. Friday night, July 30, would be opening night. Most of them left muttering that I had become odd, if not slightly deranged. I had set up a thirty-day timetable of construction to turn the vacant space into an exciting nightclub. It seemed impossible to them, especially since they were aware that I had no experience in designing, building, or operating a nightclub; but I knew it would be done.

As I walked around the space, animatedly pointing out my plans to whoever was to be involved, I could sense whether they shared my vision. Anyone involved in the project had to commit body and soul to meet the deadline. Since each subcontractor would be required to coordinate and finish his work to meet the others' schedules, we would be working around the clock. We needed teamwork.

While I supervised the construction, Ginnie concentrated on the final decorating, uniforms for the staff, and hiring employees for the opening. By the afternoon of July 30, pandemonium was breaking loose in the place. There were sixty people working feverishly to meet that evening's deadline. Carpenters were finishing final details; painters were still painting; carpeting was being laid on the floor and banquettes were being upholstered. Bar personnel, hired by Ginnie, were behind the bar stocking the liquor and filling the coolers with beer. The waitresses were lined up waiting for a seamstress who was tailoring their beige safari suit uniforms. The girls were trying on straw hats with batik bands, reminiscent of the 1940s. The club atmosphere was already starting to come together as the waitresses began to move around in their uniforms.

As the dark brown carpeting was laid out over the room, the sounds of activity became muted and the room began to look plush. The bar surface and several walls had been paneled in natural rough-sawn wood the color of sand, suggesting the desert. A truck arrived with palm trees and tropical plants from Florida. The greenery brought the room alive. Ginnie and her helpers were hanging decorative fixtures and batik fabrics throughout the club.

Meanwhile, the disc jockey began spinning records on the new sound system whose speakers were suspended over the dance floor—my own innovation. The workers began to work to the beat of the fast-paced music, determined to meet the deadline which now was only hours away. As workers broom-swept the main floor area of the club and removed all the trash and boxes, the carpet layers followed, laying the last roll right up to the entranceway. As I followed them out the door, I was shocked to find a line of hundreds of people waiting for the grand opening. We were scheduled to open in ten minutes. I turned back into the doorway almost in panic and was shocked to see a new club, completely finished, staffed, and ready to go. We had made it.

In minutes, the revelers moved past me, filling up the place. The sound system and lights were working their magic—mixing, feeding on, and creating the energy of the crowd. Cash registers ringing, ice clinking and crunching in glasses, drinks being poured. I noticed the expressions on the faces of the patrons as they looked over the new club: mouths open in wonderment. Club Marakesh had created a new level of nightlife entertainment.

I found myself standing among the crowd, still dressed in work clothes, hardly able to move, the place was so crowded. I was awestruck at the scene I had created. I made my way into a storage room where I had a new white linen suit ready for the grand opening. As I changed clothes, I heard a roar that sounded like cheering from the club, cheering you would expect to hear in a football stadium after a touchdown.

As I went back out into the club, dressed in my new linen suit, I noticed the maître d' surrounded by a crowd, all trying to give him money to get a table. A table at Marakesh had already become the hottest ticket in town. As I walked up into a seating tier where I could view the club, I realized that the roar had come from the crowd of patrons, who had stood up like a "human wave" to applaud the new club. Even above the music's loud throb, you could hear the clapping and cheering. The crowd was cheering the place itself. No doubt about it, Club Marakesh was already a hit. I felt so accomplished for creating, designing, and building the place, and I was so confident that it would be a financial success. I believed that being in the nightclub business would make me the happiest guy in the world. . . .

My life review continued. The initial success of Club Marakesh fueled my desire to build another club. While long lines of patrons were queuing up outside the doors of Marakesh for the rest of the summer of 1976, I was in New York City and Palm Beach, Florida, looking for the next site.

My relationship with Ginnie did not survive even the opening night. Before opening Marakesh, we had talked about marriage and raising a family. Ginnie wanted to have children, but I was never comfortable with the idea of such a commitment. Now the idea of raising children was inconceivable. Being in the night-club business was going to be one big party; children would only be a nuisance. Ginnie and I remained busi-ness partners but parted ways personally.

Being the owner of the hottest club in the Hamptons was an entrée for me to begin dating a series of blonde and beautiful women. I was seriously com-mitted to the nightclub business and did not want any personal relationships to interfere with my business success. Although I continued to drink heavily, I was enthusiastic about my new future in the nightclub busi-ness. Besides, I could control my drinking.

In the spring of 1978 I found a second Marakesh site in West Palm Beach. Although the space was already being operated as a sleazy nightclub, it had a large free-standing space with high ceilings in which I felt I could easily duplicate the Hamptons club. I negotiated a lease for the space in order to design and build a club for the beginning of the next winter season. I returned to the Hamptons for the summer and began to plan for con-struction of the Palm Beach club in the fall.

At that point the Hamptons Marakesh was in its third season and continued to be a smashing success. While attending a "Disco Forum" sponsored by *Billboard* magazine in June 1978, I met a real estate broker at a space that had been advertised for a nightclub in the Times Square area. The space was the recently vacated Bond store, located in a famous land-mark building on Times Square. Atop the building was the Camel cigarette sign with the huge head of a camel blowing real rings of smoke out over Times Square. The space had been an unsuccessful nightclub in the '30s and '40s. I should have read the writing on the wall.

Accompanied by the real estate broker, I entered a huge two-story lobby area with marbleized floors and a spectacular freestanding spiral art deco staircase that ascended thirty feet to the second-floor mezzanine. After ascending the staircase, we entered a spectacular space of 18,000 square feet with 35-foot-high ceilings. A separate staircase led to a higher level of 6,000 square feet that overlooked the main level from a balcony. This space alone was larger than the entire Hamptons club. Although the original nightclub space had been renovated into a retail store, much of the art deco design and ornamentation had been preserved. I was inspired by the space to consider the creation of an art deco Egyptian theme. I decided to call the Times Square location Club Pharaoh. It was one of the most magnificent spaces in Manhattan.

I envisioned that this space could be the greatest nightclub in New York City. It was twice the size of Studio 54, which was currently the city's hottest club. I was more intrigued by the architectural challenge of creating the space than the reality of trying to fill it with enough people. I was already fully committed to the Palm Beach club and was about to begin its construction in two months.

Things started moving quickly on the Times Square location with preliminary meetings with attorneys, accountants, and potential investors. Although I was eager to design and build the New York City club, I was not in a position to retain a controlling interest and assure its success. The estimated cost of building the club was more than one million dollars, an astronomical amount for a nightclub by 1978 standards. We negotiated and committed to a lease on the Times Square space without the necessary financing in place, a move which turned out to be a mistake. I was now fully committed to building nightclubs in New York City and Palm Beach at the same time—one of them to be the largest in the world and the other 1,400 miles away. It proved to be an impossible task.

I was also naive about the workings of certain businesses in New York City. Five Mafia crime families controlled the city, and one of these families controlled everything that happened in Times Square. Therefore, the Mafia became interested in my business interests. The Mafia crime family was also the subject of a massive federal investigation. Unbeknownst to me at the time, the Mafia had already taken an interest in my business success, especially in view of the potential Times Square club. Due to the investigation and surveillance of the crime family, I became a "person of interest" in the federal investigation. While I was enthusiastically going about the business of operating the Hamptons club and designing and building clubs in Palm Beach and New York City, various federal law enforcement agencies were conducting a massive investigation of the Mafia's control of legitimate businesses. They began to view me with suspicion, although I was in the dark about this.

Without my knowledge, a business associate decided to honor the Mafia's interest in the Times Square project, and a "sit-down" meeting was held at Umberto's Clam Bar on Mulberry Street in Manhattan. It was decided by a couple of thugs at this meeting that we were not going to be permitted to open at the Times Square location. I was not aware that this meeting had taken place, or that we were in jeopardy of losing the location, when the investor group backed out. As it turned out, a financial consultant who was supposedly assisting us was actually a front man for one of the

Mafia families. We were presented with a proposal of financial backing, but ultimately I would have lost everything in what amounted to being a mob-controlled scam. I was forced to walk away from the Times Square project with a considerable financial loss.

Losing Club Pharaoh significantly affected my confidence in my business judgment, so I decided to regroup from my losses. The Palm Beach club had a successful first season, and the Hamptons club was even more successful. When I returned to Palm Beach in the fall of 1979, I decided to make a major change in my life. I had been running in overdrive and focusing on my business life for three years in a row. I realized that I had very little time for myself. I decided that I should stay in Palm Beach during the winter and get to know myself better. Although my business life had been relatively successful, my personal life was devoid of any real meaning. I decided that if I slowed down my business life and got into the Palm Beach social scene, maybe I would be more successful with my personal life. It was time for a change.

I took a lease on a penthouse apartment on the Intracoastal Waterway on South Ocean Boulevard in Palm Beach across the street from a beach club filled with good-looking girls tanning themselves in bikinis while drinking piña coladas. I thought I was in seventh heaven. Day and night became a continuous party. I spent every day at the beach; dined in the evening at one of Palm Beach's trendy restaurants; and partied all night at Club Marakesh. Being the owner of the hottest nightclub in town, I easily gained access to the Palm Beach social scene, dating several of the wealthiest and most eligible women in town.

My life review began to focus on one particular scene. It was Saturday night, March 1, 1980. I was standing at my favorite spot in the Palm Beach Marakesh, the upstairs bar from where I commanded a view of the rest of the club. I wanted to be alone for a change; I had spent the previous night with two women who were heavily into the cocaine scene, which I avoided. Frankly, I didn't understand the infatuation with cocaine. Everybody in Palm Beach seemed to be doing it, including most of my friends. They claimed it made them feel sharp, brilliant, and confident; some even compared it to the B vitamins. I had been content to drink beer at the beach club during the day and champagne all night. I would drink expensive cognac if I wanted to take the edge off and get to sleep, but lately I had been drinking rum, vodka, gin, and liqueurs, looking for a change. I began to think that maybe I should start being more careful with my drinking, mindful of what had happened to my dad.

As I stood at the bar mentally addressing my concerns about my own drinking, I thought I saw the answer to my prayers walk through the front door. As this radiant young woman with long blonde hair engaged the maître d' in conversation, I remembered that I had met her briefly once before and had invited her to the club as my personal guest. I had decided she was easily the most beautiful young woman in Palm Beach. Now, as the maître d' turned and pointed in my direction, her face glowed as she recognized me.

All eyes in the crowd turned and followed her as she moved through the crowd toward me. She brushed my cheek with a kiss, and I was lost in her fragrance. As she parted from our embrace, I noticed an ornament dangling from a thin gold chain around her neck. It was a scrimshaw ivory piece carved in the shape of a fish, and the bill of the fish was carved in the shape of a small spoon, obviously for snorting cocaine. We danced until dawn and spent the next twelve days and nights together. I also spent several thousand dollars trying to keep the magic working; I couldn't get enough of her or cocaine. I had a new playmate and a new best friend. I felt brilliant, at first. Just as I began to think that maybe my drinking was getting out of control, cocaine put me back in control, or so I thought. . . .

My life review continued, as the next several years became a blur of scenes spiraling downward into a life of darkness and danger. It wasn't as if I was not in good company, to judge by the breeding, education, occupation, and financial status of those who were drawn to this affluent drug subculture I gradually slipped into. By outward appearances, the drug scene was glamorous. I had an extended group of friends from Palm Beach to Manhattan to the Hamptons. It was a prestigious group of professional people: Wall Street brokers; film, theater, and television personalities and executives; sports celebrities; models and modeling agents; artists, authors, writers, and photographers; other nightclub and restaurant owners; and other people of the night. All of my friends in this extended group had one thing in common—cocaine. In a strange way, the rituals of the cocaine experience were added to other pseudo-spiritual events in my life: drinking from the flask that passed between my dad and his friends in the cemetery, and bonding with my dad through a glass of beer.

Drug dealers became cultural icons and nightclub celebrities. Cocaine created a mystical bonding between people who would not have any reason to socialize with each other except for their mutual addictions. People who formerly had respectable reputations began to associate with the most disreputable characters such as drug dealers. It was during this time that I became even more hedonistic and materialistic, searching for the next high, the next sexual conquest, the next adrenaline adventure. By outward appearances, my life was glamorous: summers in the Hamptons, winters in Palm Beach; only the best and trendiest in travel, residences, dining; a succession of beautiful women; and constant partying.

It was during these times that I surrounded myself with many bizarre characters, including a self-professed psychic who began to influence events in my life. The psychic directed me into a "golden business opportunity" that led me into a life surrounded by crime, drugs, money-laundering, and international intrigue. I continued to maintain a role of self-preservation, just barely avoiding getting involved in anything illegal that would have ruined my lifestyle. If I followed the psychic's advice, I would not have been able to turn back from an even more dismal and dangerous future than the path I was already on.

As I viewed myself during these scenes, I realized that it was my craving for the next adrenaline adventure that led me into the crazy lifestyle I was leading. At this point, my spiritual life had fallen to its lowest ebb. It was also at this point when my angels and spirit guides apparently began to pick me up. They had a future planned for me that was different from the one I was living.

My life review, I sensed, was about to conclude. The scenes and sequences slowed to a scene where I viewed myself as a third person on a Saturday night in the spring of 1983. I was standing at my favorite spot at the upstairs bar in the Palm Beach Marakesh at the hour of critical mass. The club was already jam-packed with a good-looking crowd when the Palm Beach social set began to arrive following one of the charity balls. There were so many charity balls in Palm Beach that the social sponsors had run out of causes and diseases to which they could contribute. These charity functions were actually tax-shelter ploys, designed to allow the wealthy of Palm Beach to write off their extravagant parties.

The social set arrived in their Rolls Royces, which our valet parkers lined up in front of the club. The gentlemen entered the club in tuxedos and the women in designer gowns. Many of them were accompanied by tuxedoed security men who were employed to guard not only their employers but also the wealth of jewels that garnished the women. It was an ostentatious display of pomp and ceremony, wealth reduced to obscenity, the kind of scene that defined Palm Beach as the glamorous playground of the super-rich and elite.

By outward appearances, it was a typical Saturday night at Club Marakesh of the Palm Beaches, and by outward appearances I was my usual self at the club. I was wearing a custom-tailored designer tuxedo fitted at a Worth Avenue boutique, an expensive shirt of Egyptian cotton, hand-tied bow, black Gucci loafers, and a Rolex watch. I had easily adopted Palm Beach's standards of class.

Standing at my favorite spot, I could observe the club and each patron who came through the front door. Each time the door opened, I would turn to see who was coming in. I was waiting for the next blonde and beautiful woman who was going to walk through the door and make my life right for me. Although the club was extremely crowded, exciting, and noisy with an incredible energy level, I was standing alone and silent in the crowd. The bartender kept a bottle of Dom Perignon chilling in an ice bucket in front of me, and always kept my glass quite full. Not only did I enjoy Dom Perignon, it was a great way to lure women, to whom I would offer a glass.

Suddenly, for some reason, I found myself almost as if I was in a vacuum or a soundproof bubble; I began to have a spiritual experience. The sensation started with a roaring sound, like an ocean wave rushing past my ears. It seemed as if I was in another dimension in time and space. The music, the lights, the sounds, and the excitement seemed to recede from where I stood. The motion and movement in the club seemed to gradually slow down as if everyone around me was moving in slow motion. My senses turned inward, and I listened to the loud thumping of my heart. As I observed the patrons, each seemed to take on an aura that made them appear different on the inside from the person they were pretending to be on the outside. I watched people talking, laughing, and appearing to have a good time. But the scene before me seemed so phony, so shallow, like a facade lacking in substance and depth.

In a way, I looked beyond the surface and deeper into the people around me. I saw people laughing, who appeared to be happy on the outside, but they were crying on the inside. I saw loneliness, insecurity, fear, anxiety, searching, grasping, and clawing. I saw desperation. I saw people struggling in an environment created to be a playground that had somehow turned into an emotional battlefield. That is when I started thinking about my dad. At first, I thought, as I surveyed my nightclub empire, how proud my dad would be if he could see me at that very moment. I went through my litany of what I had, everything a single guy could want: nightclubs in the Hamptons and Palm Beach, a contemporary home in the Hamptons and a penthouse apartment in Palm Beach, a Mercedes-Benz convertible, designer clothes, the best tables at the best restaurants, plenty of money, and, of course, a Rolex watch. I became melancholy, thinking about my dad. I remembered how sad and lonely his life had become. My dad had spent his life sitting in a tavern waiting for someone to walk through the door to make things right for him.

It was sad how my dad almost had it made. It was just that one championship game, I thought, that changed Dad's luck. If it weren't for that one missed shot, his life would never have gotten out of control. If that one shot had gone through the hoop and if he had won that one championship game, everything else would have been different. We would have been a family, and growing up with him would have been so different.

However, Dad was a dreamer, and when his dream went bad he lost control. How different things were for me. I thought about the rapidly changing events in my life since I had become a nightclub entrepreneur. I wanted to have fun in this business, and at first it was fun, but then the harder I tried to have fun, the more I drank, the more I partied, the more women I was with, the less fulfilling my life became, the less I was in control. At first, long-time friends surrounded me, but then, as cocaine edged its way into the party, friends became users. The cocaine was stimulating at first. It made everyone sharper, wittier, more brilliant, but then it turned on us. At first people shared it, then they began to deal it to afford it. The deals started small, then they got bigger. Then the bad deals went down. Then came the busts and the arrests. Some people disappeared; others died. Trusting even good friends became a dangerous game. Some party!

As I stood at the bar of my own club, I wished that I could be back in my dad's tavern talking with him. He had been dead for almost nine years. If I could be talking with him, I would be happier at that very moment back in that little tavern in Hazleton than I was in the fancy nightclub I had created. I thought back to when I was driving across Nebraska after Dad had died, hearing that message so distinctly in my dad's voice. At that moment, I heard my dad's voice again, as if he were standing next to me: "He's grown up just like me! . . . My boy, he's just like me!"

I stood at the bar thinking that perhaps my dad was still alive somewhere, somehow. Maybe he was there with me in some ghostly form at that moment, watching me. I wondered if he was proud of his son, proud of what I had accomplished. But then I wondered if he was there to tell me that my life was out of control, out of sync, a crazy life, a life in turmoil, disintegrating, out of balance, a state of life that perhaps called for another way of living.

Just as suddenly as the sounds and lights had diminished and the scene had slowed down, it returned and intensified like an ocean wave and a rushing whooshing sound came past me from behind, and I was back in the reality of the nightclub scene.

I snapped out of my melancholy. It must have been something I had eaten, I thought. Perhaps I was just tired. Perhaps I was having some kind of a mental relapse, some anomaly or syndrome of thinking-gone-wrong. I decided it must have been the champagne. Perhaps I needed a change from Dom Perignon. I instructed the bartender to open a bottle of Perrier Jouet for a change. Then I looked down at the long-stem champagne flute in my hand. I noticed that I had been turning the glass in my hand counterclockwise, around and around. It was a habit I had developed unconsciously. I continued to think about my life, and the glass continued to turn counterclockwise in my hand. *I'm just like my dad,* I thought, as my life review ended.

CHAPTER 9

THE LADY OF LIGHT

A great sign appeared in the sky:
A woman clothed with the sun, and the
moon was under her feet, and upon
her head a crown of twelve stars.

Revelation 12:1

As my life review ended, I found myself still suspended within the crystalline sphere. Surrounding me
in every direction was an incredible vastness of space.
Stars and planets in varying degrees of brilliance seemed
to stretch into infinity. The universe in which these
stars and planets existed was in a realm of indescribable
depth. I realized that I was not in the universe as I knew
it on Earth, but in another celestial realm. I became
aware that the universe in which Earth is located is only
part of a more limitless heavenly realm.

Suddenly, I found myself standing in a beautiful
garden setting. As I marveled at this incredible setting of
nature, a brilliant light appeared in the garden. I found

myself in the presence of a beautiful, radiant, and angelic being, dressed in white with a veil that covered her head and flowed to the bottom of her full-length gown. A lighter veil covered her face, which was not fully visible. The light that radiated from her was of a heavenly brilliance that prevented me from fully observing her, but she was beautiful.

She became known to me as the Lady of Light, and she radiated golden light far brighter and of a much greater magnitude than the light of any of the other angelic or spiritual beings I had seen. Clearly, the Lady of Light held a very high place in the spiritual hierarchy. She began to communicate with me. Her manner was eloquent and soft-spoken, yet the tone of her message was serious. The Lady of Light waved her right arm, and I watched as scenes, as if in a movie, developed before me. I became aware that I was watching future events of my life, scenes that were incongruent with the life that I had been living so far.

The Lady of Light showed me scenes where I was writing manuscripts, researching materials and books, and embarking on a lifelong quest for truth and knowledge. The Lady of Light told me that I would begin by writing a book about my experiences and that my book would become a source of inspiration for many people in search of their true spiritual nature. The Lady of Light showed me that I would become involved in research in college and university settings. I was shown a future scene in a university auditorium in which I was conducting a seminar. As I watched myself speaking from the stage in this future scene, I stood to the side of the auditorium with the Lady of Light. I watched as I was apparently addressing an audience of doctors, medical researchers, and students. As I absorbed this scene, I thought the Lady of Light must have had me confused with someone else. I could not imagine why doctors, medical researchers, and students would possibly have had any interest in anything I had to say.

In an even more incongruous scene, I saw myself in Washington, D.C., dressed in a conservative business suit and walking through the halls of the United States Congress and Senate buildings. I saw myself meeting with political leaders and addressing them from a podium in an auditorium setting.

I saw myself becoming involved in the film industry. I was involved in the direction of a movie scene being filmed in my childhood neighborhood. I seemed to have developed a sense of wanting to communicate very important ideas to others and that the film, television, and media outlets provided the means for me. I saw that my convictions and beliefs and the messages I was trying to communicate would become the subjects of much criticism. I knew that I was going to be criticized, discredited, and vilified by individuals and organizations that felt threatened by what I had to say. I recognized that these organizations and individuals, many of whom were well-meaning, were motivated more by fear and loss of control than by their willingness to be open-minded and accepting of spiritual beliefs.

I watched scene after scene of my visits at the bedsides of sick and dying people, both young and old. It seemed that I had developed insights that were comforting to those who were facing sickness and death. I saw that I became a different person when I was making these visits. The experience of being with people who were sick and dying was rewarding for me as well as for them. I recognized that the greatest rewards in life do not come from seeking material riches and physical comfort, but from performing acts of caring and kindness for others.

I watched scenes of my being involved in directing and coordinating the distribution of food and supplies to people who were hungry or in need. Although my efforts were initially limited to small groups of people, I saw that the need for the distribution of food supplies to needy people would grow tremendously. I saw that certain world events would alter the availability and distribution of food supplies and that worldwide hunger would become a massive problem. During this worldwide crisis, I saw that there was still an abundance of food in the world to feed all of its inhabitants. In fact, there was always an abundance of food despite the fact that many men, women, and children were dying of starvation. However, the greed and avarice of those in control of the supplies prevented the food from being adequately distributed.

I saw myself traveling extensively, conducting seminars. Many of my travels involved expeditions to the ruins of ancient civilizations in a quest for knowledge and truths that were to be found in the lessons of past civilizations. Much of our future and the future events of the world itself were to be found in the clues that had been left by past civilizations on earth.

I was shown that at some point in my future life I was going to create a foundation called Mission of Angels. I was given specific goals that were to be achieved by this foundation. One of the goals of the Mission of Angels Foundation was to create a spiritual center. I was shown a facility that resembled a large country inn in an idyllic setting that was to be utilized as the location for the spiritual center.

Although I saw that I would become deeply involved and passionate in my lifelong work, I was also saddened by the knowledge that my work and my travels would distance me from family and friends. My writings would require many long hours of solitude, but I was inspired by the awareness that I would eventually be rewarded for the fruits of my labor.

As the movie-like scenes of my future life ended, I found myself in a building, which became known to me as the Hall of Records. I was sitting on a marble bench and waiting. From there I could look outdoors through a large opening at the side of the room. I could see columns of large pillars supporting an archway of the building in which I sat. In front of the columns, there was a long stairway leading to a large open courtyard. I sensed that I was in this great and magnificent structure on earth, only during another time period. The architecture and design of the building led me to conclude that this place was probably in ancient Egypt. However, as I did not see any other beings or human activity I concluded I was still in the celestial realm.

The Lady of Light appeared in the room before me. She stood next to a large globe of Earth, which was suspended in a large circular frame attached to the marble floor. The Lady of Light began to speak to me about the future of the world as she pointed to the globe. I watched as she pointed to the Middle East, and I saw a flashpoint of light. She then pointed to Italy, and I saw another flashpoint. Then flashpoints broke out rapidly throughout the Middle East and Europe representing major incidents, world events caused by mankind: acts of aggression, terrorism, and war. Fanatical, self-proclaimed religious groups supposedly acting in the name of God performed many of these acts, but I was told that acts of war and aggression were not part of God's plan.

I was shown a vision of a large plateau in the Middle East. The plateau was surrounded by a dusty, dry, and barren region that seemed to be deserted and devoid of any life. I was told that future events at this location in the Middle East would start a chain reaction of man-made catastrophic events, first in the Middle East, then in Africa and Europe, followed by events in Russia and China.

The Lady of Light showed me another scene of Earth suspended in space. I watched as the axis of Earth's rotation began to shift significantly. I could not tell how much time the shift took, nor was I shown a time or date when it would take place. I could tell that significant geophysical changes to the Earth's surface would take place as a result of the shifting of Earth's axis. Great earthquakes erupted throughout the world, significantly changing the major continents. There were volcanic eruptions of great magnitude spewing clouds of billowing smoke and ash throughout the atmosphere, sending the Earth into a period of darkness. Great floods resulted from melting and shifting polar ice caps. Many low-lying land areas were engulfed by huge tidal waves. I watched scenes of these events taking place, depicted like black and white movies. I watched one scene from a hilltop location on the coastline of Long Island, New York, as rows of massive tidal waves descended on the coastline, burying the land under the water. I saw another scene from a street corner in New York City. A wall of water rushed down the wide street as surrounding office buildings began to collapse. In another scene, I watched as a massive wall of water hit the coastline of Miami Beach. In its wake, I watched as an entirely new land mass rose up out of the ocean.

The Lady of Light told me that none of these future events would have to take place if mankind began to recognize and work with God's plan.

The Lady of Light told me: "The way to understand and work with God's plan is through prayer and meditation, through prayer to call to God, and through meditation to receive His message."

I was told that the world could be saved, not by its leaders, but by prayer groups throughout the world. I was told that the prayers of a group of twenty could save a nation from war. I was told that the fate of mankind rested on our ability, individually and collectively, to change the direction of mankind in accordance with God's plan.

CHAPTER 10

THE MAGNIFICENT MAN

The scenes before me suddenly dissolved, and I found myself back in the original garden setting. Beyond the garden was a vastness of space, and beyond it yet, a very earthly scene of a mountainside and valley that I recognized as a location on planet Earth.

As I acclimated myself to the surroundings, I saw before me an incredible-looking being. The Magnificent Man, as I like to call him, was seated in the garden in a serene and peaceful setting. He was wearing a white flowing robe, shimmering and shining as if made from the finest silk. He had long-flowing and slightly curling auburn hair and a closely trimmed beard. His eyes were not visible to me, as he was attending to a small group of toddlers who surrounded him playfully. I focused my attention on two of the children who were to the right of the group. They drew my attention because they had turned to look at me. Although I perceived that one was a boy and the other a girl, I noticed more particularly their identical appearances. Later, I would understand that they were twins. There were several other toddlers surrounding the Magnificent Man. As I focused my attention on each of them, the children looked directly and longingly toward me as if they were seeking some acknowledgment or understanding from me. I perceived that I should have known these children, but the scene confused me.

The Lady of Light became visible to me as she entered the garden from the right. She was now more clearly visible to me, for she no longer wore the veil covering her head and concealing her face from me. She had long-flowing, dark auburn hair that careened over her shoulders. She wore a golden crown, simple in design. She was, as I originally perceived, the most beautiful woman I have ever seen. I conveyed to the Lady of Light that I needed to understand the scene before me and that I was confused by it. The Lady of Light responded by introducing me to another scene. I became fully involved as a participant in this scene, filled with love, joy, and pride. I was standing with a group of people I did not immediately recognize, except for a handsome young man dressed in a cap and gown. The scene was on an academic campus, and it was a bright, sunny, and glorious day. I was filled with love, joy, and pride for the young man who was celebrating his graduation.

I was quickly back in the garden setting and filled with questions. I conveyed to the Lady of Light that I wanted to know the meaning of this vision. I did not have any children; nor did I plan on having children. I thought of children as an inconvenience and a nuisance. They had no place in my life as far as I was concerned.

I was perplexed by my reaction to the scene of the young man at his graduation. During that moment, I experienced emotions that I had never known before, emotions of love, joy, and pride that only a father could know. But I was not a father. I did not have any children. The prospect of such a long-term commitment was frightening to me. As I conveyed those thoughts and emotions, the group of children surrounding the Magnificent Man slowly vanished, disappearing before my eyes. I immediately felt an excruciating loss, a terrible and heart-wrenching pain. I was feeling the pain of the loss of these children.

Then I realized who these children were. During my earthly life, opportunities to have children were presented to me on a number of occasions. Since I perceived that these children would be inconveniences in my life, I chose not to have children—these children who were the focus of the Magnificent Man's attention. They were the children in spirit of the souls that were intended to be my children during my life. They were opportunities that I had decided were inconveniences.

I pondered the scene before me, now absent of the children, for what seemed like an interminable period of time. Then a small boy appeared in the garden from the direction of the Lady of Light. The beautiful small boy was immediately drawn to the Magnificent Man, who reached out with his left arm and hand to greet the boy in a protective and loving manner. The little boy was strong and full of life. He had blond hair that was almost golden and the biggest blue eyes I have ever seen on a little boy. I perceived that the Magnificent Man was showing the little boy to me in a protective manner because I also would be given an opportunity in the future to protect a little boy. I perceived that this little boy was to be that opportunity.

I turned to the Lady of Light and conveyed to her that I wanted to know who this little boy was and what was the significance of the scene before me. I didn't have children; I didn't anticipate having children. Was this little boy to be my son? The Lady of Light responded, "Truly he is a son of God!"

As she communicated that thought, the little boy disappeared from my view. As the Magnificent Man arose from his place and moved away from the garden, he appeared to be suspended in the vastness of space. He was facing in my direction as he moved away. I could now see his full figure dressed in the white robe with a vertical burgundy stripe down the center. Once he was visible to me in full figure with his arms outstretched from his sides, I perceived that he wanted to convey to me important events, lessons for me to learn, and messages for me to absorb for my return to my life.

A flood of questions raced through my mind as I was shown events that I understood were to take place on Earth in the future, during the "End Times." I was aware of the presence of the Lady of Light, visible to my right, viewing the scenes that were before me. I realized that the Lady of Light was also influencing my viewing of the scenes of the End Times. As I focused on her, I recognized her place and prominence in the sequence of events that were to take place during the End Times. I was aware that the earthly landscape of mountainside and valley was visible beyond the vastness of space that represented the End Times. In other words, I was being shown an earthly landscape that would exist following the End Times. I recognized that the End Times did not mean the end of the world. It meant the end of the world as we know it, but it also meant the beginning of a new world. I perceived that the earthly landscape in the distance was part of the new world, but it seemed so far away—barely discernible, almost mystical, like a dream world.

The Lady of Light waved her right hand in the direction of the earthly landscape and drew my attention to it. The view appeared to telescope toward me. The mountainside and valley scene was familiar, and I again recognized the scene from an actual location on Earth. However, I was now viewing this scene at a time that was several decades after the year 2000. This garden setting in which I stood had been transformed during the intervening years by great geophysical changes to the earth. It was now located in a clearing on a field of grass of incredible richness and texture. I was surrounded by trees of pine, birch, and spruce, but they were interspersed incongruously with smaller tropical plants and bushes, and the trees, plants, and bushes seemed to have a life of their own. The roots, trunks, branches, and leaves of the plants and trees had a life force of energy coursing through them; even the blades of grass seemed to be vibrantly alive. All things had energy and life in this place and were all interconnected by some greater design and source of energy. It seemed as if all the plant life was communicating an energy, an energy of life. I absorbed this energy willingly, recognizing that the energy of this place had special healing powers that I wanted to absorb. I felt that I was one with nature, and that everything in nature, whether animate or inanimate in appearance, consisted of a universal energy that was meant to be shared.

The climate of this location was now warmer than I remembered it, which accounted for the tropical plants interspersed with the pine, birch, and spruce trees. Furthermore, the sky was now more brilliant and of a different coloring as a result of the preceding Earth changes. I recognized that nature was now in harmony with God's plan, and that God's influence on Earth could be seen and manifested by observing all things in nature.

The Lady of Light directed my attention to the mountainside and the valley. I recognized a home I saw in a clearing on the side of the mountain. I then found myself viewing a scene in a second-floor bedroom inside the house. I watched as an elderly man was peacefully and serenely preparing to die. His son was standing at the foot of his bed. It was one of those special moments between a father and a son that they would both remember for eternity. They were communicating to each other that they had had a wonderful life together although they had to endure many hardships. But at this moment they shared feelings of love and joy that could only exist between a parent and child. There was no sadness between them, for the act of dying was no longer viewed with sadness and fear. In this new era of mankind, death was accepted and recognized for what it truly is, the transitional process between the soul's journey on Earth and the spiritual afterlife. It was one of the many changes that separated the new world from the old. It was a brave new world in which the father and son lived, and it assured me that this world has a wonderful future.

CHAPTER 11

THE RETURN

As the visions of the future ended, the crystalline sphere suddenly dissolved. I was still standing on the celestial field of the amphitheater. I remembered that the scenes taking place in the crystalline sphere were viewed by the thousands of spiritual beings now standing in silence, directing their attention toward me. It was a period of reflection, time for me to absorb the enormity of the scenes presented to me. There are no secrets in the spiritual realms. Every event that had taken place in my life, every event in my future, was known to the spiritual beings. However, I sensed that much of what had taken place in the past and what was to take place in the future depended on my participation as a human and spiritual being. In both realms, I had the gift of free will to choose my own destiny. How I chose to exercise my free will would continue to change or alter the course of my future destiny, just as it affected my past.

The stillness of the amphitheater seemed interminable. I viewed the spiritual beings more closely, scanning the crowded amphitheater. I found myself communicating with each being. I was looking to each for direction or a response. As I looked at each spirit while communicating my bewilderment, I got a response. I did not recognize the response at first. I was looking for more concrete answers. I was asking, "What now? Where do I go from here?"

As I completed this scan, my attention was drawn to my right, to the group of family members and friends that I recognized more closely from both my spiritual and earthly life. As I looked at them quizzically, they communicated their response, just as all the other spiritual beings did. The answer was uniform: "The performance of your mission in life is up to you."

Once again, my friend and guide, Dan, was at my side. As I continued to face the amphitheater and the thousands of silent spiritual beings, we began to drift backward across the field and away from the amphitheater. I felt as if I was leaving home on a long journey—on a mission—but I sensed I would return.

Suddenly, the thousands of spiritual beings began to cheer in unison, and their cheering reached me like a wave of wind. I felt this powerful energy wave pour through me as Dan and I continued to withdraw from the amphitheater. The wave of energy transformed itself into a symphony of farewell and support as they again communicated to me, "You are doing wonderfully. We are here to support you. Continue to do good work. We will help you. You are part of us and we are part of you. We stand ready to come to your aid when you need us, and you will. Call us. Beckon us. We will flock to you when the time comes."

Dan and I began to drift down through the stars. It seemed as if my consciousness had been altered during this period of time because I sensed that we were drifting back down to Earth, yet I didn't experience traveling through light years of space going this way.

The stars were suddenly not as bright, and I sensed that we were in Earth's atmosphere. I saw the outline of a wooded hillside to my right, dotted with lights that twinkled as we moved down. Then I saw the outlines of buildings in a small city and the streets below. I recognized the taller buildings as being in downtown Hazleton.

Dan and I were floating down over Donegal Hill. I recognized the spires of St. Gabriel's Church as we floated by them. We continued to float down until we were suspended just above the asphalt surface of Elm Street. We paused there for a quiet and peaceful moment as we gazed at my grandmother's home. The night was now dark and still; no one could be seen on the street. It was a moment of serenity and recollection for me. As I lingered there relishing the moment, I was at peace.

Suddenly, the dark night vanished and was instantly replaced by a brilliant summer day with a deep-blue, cloudless sky. However, the light that radiated through this scene was the light of God. I felt myself and everything around me being embraced by His light. I felt peace, contentment, and joy. I felt God's love being radiated through all of His creation. Dan and I were still suspended over Elm Street, but everything before us seemed to be brand new. Each home and building had rich detail, radiant and brilliant. The trees, shrubs, bushes, and privet hedges were alive with color. Flowers bloomed majestically before us in the nearby gardens. The lawns were alive. Each blade of grass was part of a vast, unified chorus moving in harmony with great peace. Birdsong richly filled the air, each tone seeming like a symphony. The air was filled with a rich fragrance.

I contemplated the scene before me and pondered its significance. Although I was viewing an earthly place of which I had fond memories, it had been transformed into a heavenly vision as the light of God radiated through it. I had learned from my journey that God's heavenly realms have many levels beyond our universe. Now I recognized that God's light could even turn this place on Earth into a heavenly place. I saw that my perception of heaven and Earth was changing. Although I was viewing my childhood neighborhood which seemed, at first glance, aged and shabby, God enabled me to see the scenes through His eyes as a place of wonderment and beauty.

I was most affected by my awareness of the energy that permeated all matter. This spiritual energy was a confirmation of God's presence in all levels of existence. I recognized that all material things, no matter how inanimate or insignificant to the eye, are influenced by an energy from the Creator. In a spiritual state of existence, I could see the uniqueness of all things, that all particles of existence are directed and controlled by a spiritual energy created by God to regulate the universe. As a spiritual being viewing my childhood neighborhood, I could indeed view "Heaven on Earth" in everything before me.

I wondered if I would retain this ability to see things differently when I returned to my earthly life. Would I recognize God's presence in all creation, even in the simplest things like a flower, a blade of grass, a drop of water? Could other humans see things differently, as I did at this moment?

My journey thus far had prepared me to remember that it was within God's plan to radiate a life force throughout the world. I knew that it was part of God's plan to radiate the light of God throughout the planet at some future date, so that all of humanity would have the opportunity to recognize God's existence in Earth's reality. Was I being shown what the future of Earth would be like following implementation of God's plan?

I tried to communicate my thoughts to Dan, but I didn't get any answers. Dan pointed toward my grandmother's house and smiled. "I wanted to bring you back here to your old neighborhood. You must remember this experience. This is not a dream. There is much ahead of you, and you will need to remember this experience to perform your mission in life. We are back on Earth now. It is time for you to go back to the place where we started this journey."

I started to protest. I wasn't ready to go back. I had too many questions. There was too much to be learned. I realized that my journey was about to end, but I wanted it to last forever.

I felt the warmth and vibrancy of God's light pulsing through my being. I was without pain or suffering, which I had left behind in my human body. Yet, I also now felt that God's light was preparing me—anesthetizing me—for my return to my body. As Dan turned to face me directly for the first time since the beginning of our journey, I realized it was time to go back. Certainly, I was already back on earth, in Hazleton, but I was there in a spiritual realm, not in a physical form. It was time for me to reenter my body and return to my earthly existence.

Dan communicated a final message to me: "Relax. Everything will be okay. It's time for you to go." He reached out and gently pushed me backwards. I was still filled with the brilliant light of God as I floated away from him. As I drifted backwards, the brilliant light began to fade; the warm and loving glow that filled my being turned to darkness. At first, my descent was slow and soft, but suddenly it became quick and violent. I felt as if I was being hurled out of heaven and back into my physical body.

As I found myself reunited with my flesh, a painful jolt of electricity exploded in my chest. It was the most excruciating pain I have ever experienced. Suddenly, it was incredibly cold, and I was in darkness. I realized I was back in my body, trapped in it. A primordial scream started deep inside me. It was a scream that consumed all the energy I could muster to release the pain I was feeling. It was a scream released into total darkness, into a black void. I was the only one who heard it.

"We got him this time!" the paramedic exclaimed. I had been successfully resuscitated, but the emergency medical technicians continued to work feverishly on me. The EMTs sighed in relief as my vital signs were restored, but their job was not over yet. At this point, no one was watching the clock, but a long period of time had elapsed during the ambulance trip, when I appeared to have been lost. A strange and eerie presence seemed to permeate the ambulance during that time. Although those present in the ambulance sensed it, it wouldn't be discussed until much later. The ambulance crew members were well-trained and dedicated volunteers. They used all their experience, skill, and knowledge to revive me. Nothing else mattered.

I was momentarily aware that I was back in the ambulance, gagging on a device that had been inserted into my throat to enable the EMTs to conduct artificial respiration. They had brought me back. I should have had the greatest appreciation for their efforts, yet I didn't because I didn't want to be there! Although the EMTs restored my breathing, I was suffocating. I was a spiritual being stuffed into a human body. I was no longer able to float free. I had limitations of thought and movement. I could now feel suffering and pain, anger and hate. I was a human again. I felt myself collapse into unconsciousness as the ambulance sped down the dark highway to the hospital.

PART II

THE RECOVERY

Some fell by laudanum (opium),
and some by steel (scalpel),
And death in ambush lay in every pill!
                    —*Sir Samuel Garth, physician and poet*

CHAPTER 12

THE HOSPITAL EXPERIENCE

July 2, 1984, 11:27 P.M.

> Some near-death survivors feel as if they "were kicked out of heaven," reviving as they did when they actually wanted to stay. Most of them know they are not as perfect as it seems like they ought to be, considering where they went. None claim sainthood. States of depression can be lengthy, the experience seeming as much a curse as a blessing.
> —*P. M. H. Atwater*

I was admitted into the emergency room of the hospital at 11:27 P.M. Approximately one hour and six minutes had elapsed from the time I collapsed on the sidewalk. During that time, I was in various stages of cardiac and/or respiratory arrest. The emergency room physician listed the admitting diagnosis as respiratory arrest although I began breathing on my own during the admission procedures.

A loud buzzing sound was ringing in my ears. I was aware of being in an antiseptic, white-tiled room. I instantly knew that I was back in my body; it was racked with pain. I could not open my eyes because I was blinded by the harshness of the light. I was aware that beings in white were ministering to someone in a bed next to mine. I was trying to be positive about the place I was in; I was in denial that I could possibly be back on Earth and not in some heavenly place.

I thought the buzzing sound was the noise created by some kind of jigsaw that the beings in white were using on the person in the bed next to me. I assured myself that they were cutting away the carcass of this person, so the spirit could be detached from it. Although the pain of being back in my body was excruciating, I convinced myself that they were going to release me from my carcass also, so I could continue my celestial journey. I was theorizing that this was some kind of heavenly wayside station and that somehow I had been returned to my body by mistake. Soon the beings in white would begin to work on me, and I would again be free of my body. The possibility of remaining permanently stuffed back into a physical body was too frightening to bear.

I was in a semi-comatose state, but I became somewhat aware that the beings in white were doctors and nurses who were now surrounding my bed. Apparently I had been mumbling, "I love everyone! . . . Who are you? . . . I love you!"

I continued mumbling, "Am I dead? . . . Am I dying? . . . Is this heaven?" The doctors and nurses listened to my semi-comatose ramblings and concluded that I was probably a drug overdose patient.

I was certain that I was surrounded by spiritual beings who were going to release me from my human carcass—my gorilla suit—and allow me to continue on my celestial journey. Instead, hospital personnel, who did not have the slightest idea why I was so confused, surrounded me. I was lapsing in and out of a semi-comatose state, hoping to return to heaven, when an ear-piercing voice echoed through my head. It was an earthly female voice, vile-sounding and loathsome, interrupting my peaceful journey. It was definitely not the voice of the Lady of Light.

"What drugs are you on?" The voice was booming through my brain.

"What drugs?" I responded, trying to open my eyes, but blinded by the light.

"What drugs did you take? You overdosed on drugs. We need to know what drugs you are on in order to treat you."

"Where am I?" I stammered, thinking "hell" would be the reply.

"You are in the hospital," the nurse replied impatiently. "In the emergency room. You have been admitted for a drug overdose. We need to know what drugs you are on in order to treat you."

Was this a bad dream? Did I dream that I was in heaven and now I had moved on to hell? Wherever I was, I did not want to become fully conscious. The reality of being back on earth, back in my body, and in a hospital, was terrifying. I tried to slip back into my other reality, but the voice became more insistent as its owner started to shake me by the arm, urging me to awaken.

"We need to know what drugs you are on, or we can't help you. We may have to pump your stomach!"

Now that was a serious threat. I tried to open my eyes to deal with this wretched-sounding woman, but the light was too intense and blinding. I blinked to adjust my eyes, but my eyes were too sensitive to the light. I began to realize that I was going to have to protect myself and deal with these threats.

"What happened to me?" I mumbled, expecting an answer that would explain everything.

The nurse rambled on, screaming at me only inches from my ear, telling me that I was on drugs.

"I didn't take any drugs!" I became more lucid, recognizing the threat. "I don't know what happened. I remember feeling an electrical explosion in my head and then I collapsed, but I did not take any drugs!"

I tried to recall the events that had preceded my arrival at the hospital. I could remember spending a relaxed afternoon with my friends, then going to the club, and the altercation, followed by an exploding feeling in my head, and collapsing on the sidewalk. But my recall of these events was hazy and fragmented. I was overwhelmed by other recollections that were unbelievable, beyond my imagination. The ineffable journey from which I had just returned was of far more importance to me than the conditions that concerned the doctors and nurses.

I vividly recalled the experience: leaving my body in the ambulance, the greeting from Dan, the tunnel of energy, envelopment by the light. I began to relive the experience in detail as the medical staff continued to observe my supposedly confused state of mind. I must have been mumbling about what I had experienced because the same nurse was at my side, screaming in my ear, "If you don't stop talking that nonsense, we are going to call the psychiatrist!"

Now that was an even more serious threat. I realized that I was lying helplessly in a hospital bed, stuck with needles, hooked up to machines. I wasn't capable of moving, escaping, or defending myself. I had just returned from an experience in another realm of existence, and I wanted to talk about it. My experience was real and true for me, but I had never heard of anyone having any experience like it. I wanted to hear from these medical professionals that they understood what had happened to me. However, the threat of bringing in the psychiatrist warned me to put up a protective wall of silence. I was obviously being treated as a drug overdose patient in a confused state of mind. I realized I had better stop talking.

I had to deal with the accusation that I had overdosed on drugs. Although I was a product of the '60s and '70s, by choice I was not a drug user. When many of my friends were smoking pot, popping pills, or taking LSD, I was content to confine my mood-altering drugs primarily to alcohol. My experience with other drugs was limited and unsatisfactory. I was Irish Catholic; drinking was my drug of choice, except for cocaine. However, cocaine had become history for me by this time. Although I did use it for several years, mostly to attract women, I had not used cocaine since February 1983. It was now July 1984. It had been at least sixteen months since I had used cocaine or any other drug, legal or illegal. If I had been on drugs, the doctors could possibly have almost convinced me that what I had experienced was a hallucination or a figment of my imagination. But such an explanation would fall far short of acceptable. I could not dismiss this experience—it would just not go away.

As I lay in the hospital bed, I tested myself. Could I be wrong? I tried to erase the experience from my memory, but I could not. This spiritual experience happened. It was more real than reality. It was a true experience. No matter how hard I tried to deny it, I couldn't. I began to think back to the previous night's events.

The surges of adrenaline I had felt before collapsing may have spread through my bloodstream to my brain, releasing endorphins and causing a euphoric flight of fancy. However, no amount of adrenaline pumping through my system—and my heart wasn't even pumping—could have awakened me in the ambulance when I was without vital signs. Adrenaline surges could not explain how I viewed the ambulance attendants working on my body from a position outside of it. No rush of endorphins could have lifted me out of the ambulance and propelled me through the tunnel of energy. Certainly, no chemical substance lying dormant in my body could have reformulated itself and rushed to my brain creating the image of Dan McCampbell; nor could it explain everything else that I had experienced. The electrical shock I felt as I was resuscitated in the ambulance may have restored me physically to my body, but it could not explain the celestial journey from which I had just returned. A force more powerful than anything available to the EMTs in the ambulance had orchestrated that journey.

During the early morning hours following my admission, the attending physician ordered that I remain in the intensive care unit for observation. Since I was being treated for a possible drug overdose, no sedation was permitted. IVs had been inserted in my arm, and a cardiac monitor was attached to my torso. Chest X-rays and an EKG were ordered.

Later in the morning, I became more conscious and aware that I was in the intensive care unit of a hospital. I was awake and in my body, in pain, angry, and confused. Mostly, I was troubled by the lights and hospital noise. I kept my eyes closed as much as possible to block out the light and to escape back into a dream world, attempting to deny that I was in a hospital. Although years of nightclub clamor had dulled my sensitivity to sound, the noise of the activity in the hospital seemed deafening. Simple low-level conversations between the doctors and nurses were irritating. Somehow, the journey from which I had just returned had affected my sensitivity to light and sound, but I didn't understand why.

By midday I was assigned a physician. I preferred anyone to the admitting doctor who had me being treated as a drug overdose case. When my physician approached the bed to read the chart, I noticed that he was not wearing hospital whites. Instead, he appeared to be wearing tennis whites. He kept checking his watch, and I sensed that he was on his way to the tennis courts after his hospital rounds, and was concerned about missing his tennis game. I realized that it was the July Fourth holiday week, not a good time to be stuck in a hospital for either doctor or patient.

My physician took his place next to my bed with the clipboard in hand, turning and flipping the pages. I assumed that he would tell me the bad news, exactly what had happened to me, when he finished reading the charts. I knew that I had come close to losing my life, that I had visited death, and that it was not a time to play games with the doctor. Besides, I liked this doctor's demeanor and was prepared to be honest with him and assist him in any way that I could. I knew that the question of drugs was going to come up. I stopped thinking about the experience. I was now very much in an earthly environment. I had to deal with what had happened to me physically, and I thought that my physician would have all the answers.

"The records indicate that you were in pretty bad shape when they brought you into the emergency room. The ambulance records say you were in respiratory arrest; they almost lost you in the ambulance. Can you tell me what happened?" He looked at me with concern, perhaps accusingly.

"Look, Doc," I responded, "all I can remember is that I was involved in an altercation in the club. Right after that, I had trouble breathing. I thought I heard my lungs collapse and my heart stop beating. I felt an explosion in my head and then I blanked out. When I became aware that I was in an emergency room, some nurse was screaming to me that I was on drugs, and that is just not the truth. I realize I was in pretty bad shape when I got here. I'm certainly not going to hide anything from you now."

He looked at me blankly. I was sure that he had seen many drug overdoses before, and that most of them were in denial and claimed not to be on drugs. Why should I be treated differently? Why should he believe me? Somehow, I knew he didn't. "The admission notes indicate that you had been taking coke for two days prior to being admitted." He looked at me accusingly.

"That's a lie!" I responded angrily. "No friend would have said that. What is his name, if he claims to be a friend?"

My physician flipped through the sheets on the clipboard, looking for a name. I sensed that he was disappointed. "We don't have a name here, but we will have to check it out. In the meantime, we are going to have to go with what we have. I'll be ordering some tests. You'll be here for observation for a few days."

He signed the papers transferring me to his care as a patient, while ordering additional tests and reports. I requested and was assigned a private room. I had a lot to think about, and I wanted to do it privately.

I awoke Tuesday evening in a room that was dark and quiet. As I had requested, the curtains and shades had been drawn on the windows. I felt secure in the private room; I didn't want any interruptions. I wanted to process this experience, this real and true event. I recalled the journey starting with the explosion in my head—like an electrical short circuit searing my brain—then falling to the ground, continuing to fall fully conscious into the black void and stillness. I recalled awakening in the ambulance, sitting up, perplexed that no one could hear me. I recalled hearing the urgency in the EMTs' voices: "No vital signs!" "The patient has coded!" Bill, sitting next to the driver: "Oh, God, no! Come on, Ned, you've got to make it! Don't give up now! You've got to make it!" Then I remembered being up and out of my body, out of the ambulance, and thinking, *Wow, this is something new. Wait until I tell my friends about this experience.*

But I wouldn't tell anyone. No one would believe it. This event—this experience, whatever it was—would have to stay with me for a long time. I needed to analyze it, to deal with it, and I didn't want any earthly interruptions while I was doing so.

Even so, I was constantly awakened and interrupted from reliving the experience by the nurses performing their routines. I responded angrily to their interference and they noted my disposition on the medical charts: "Patient appears to be in a confused state. . . . Sleeping, refuses lunch and family visits. . . . Wants to know why he passed out, complains of back pain and discomfort. . . . Patient is agitated and upset."

Confused? Agitated? Upset? You can believe I was! I didn't know what happened to me physically. Did I have a heart attack or some kind of brain seizure? The doctors and nurses gave me no answers. Agitated and upset? I didn't want to be lying on my back, in pain, in a hospital room. Only hours before, I felt like I was in the prime of my life. I had everything to live for. Everything had been going my way. All of a sudden, I was lying in a hospital bed. How could this happen to me?

I had an experience completely beyond my comprehension. I had just returned from a celestial out-of-body experience and I wanted to return to it. I wanted to float free from my body and return to the heavens, and I couldn't do it. I was trapped—and agitated and upset.

I awoke early on Wednesday, July 4, after a period of vivid dreams. It was still dark outside my room. I kept reexperiencing the trip in the ambulance, and the trip up and out of the ambulance. As I relived each part of the experience, the events became more vivid, more detailed. Unlike normal dreams, which I usually remembered after waking and then forgot, these events became more real as I reviewed them. Recalling the experience was like watching a videotape with a remote control, except that the VCR was in my brain and my memory was the videotape. Reviewing each step of the experience, I could fast-forward to one segment or rewind it to another part.

I was overwhelmed by a realization. My brain was functioning differently. It was processing information differently from how it had before I had this experience. It seemed as if a fog had been lifted from my capacity to reason and analyze. I found myself analyzing each event and recognizing its significance. There was nothing conveyed to me during this experience that did not have importance or relevance in my past and present life, except for events that were shown to me as being part of my future. The Lady of Light had shown me future events in my life that could not possibly involve me. Although past and present events in my life were accurately recorded, I decided that someone must have gotten me confused with somebody else when I was shown my future life.

When I was shown my past and present life in more vivid detail than I could possibly remember, and when I was shown things that had happened around me that I could not possibly have known, that confirmed for me that this was not a hallucination, dream, or fantasy. These were real and true events in my past, combined with an analysis of why they had taken place. All the past events and why they had happened were made known to me in a perfect way. But these future events must be hallucinations, dreams, or fantasies. Besides, I was in denial that I was even back on planet Earth in a hospital. I was trying to convince myself that the spiritual beings were going to come back for me very soon, maybe any minute, any day, but they wouldn't take long. I theorized that what I had experienced was an orientation program. I was convinced that I was going to die again soon and return to the world of spirit. So all those future events must have been part of some other person's life.

I found myself riding on a high-speed roller coaster of emotions. I was going up, down, and all over the place emotionally, going through denial, anger, bargaining, depression, and acceptance. I no longer feared death; I was in fear of living. If I were to believe the future events in my life that I had been shown, it meant that I was going to live a much longer life. However, I couldn't imagine how I was going to do it, because I didn't want to go back to my old life. As I lay in the dark room, panic and nausea overcame me. I decided to go back into meditation, to escape the hospital room and return to the experience.

While in a deep meditation or dream state, I viewed a panoramic landscape of lush, tropical foliage in a foreign land. I looked out over fields surrounded by jungle. Far in the distance, dark plumes of smoke billowed from majestic mountains. Thunderous rumbles rolled across the sky, echoing from the distant hills. Suddenly, a roar, a whirling noise, and wind flew over me, and then another, and another. Military helicopters were swooping down, hovering over a clearing. My first sense was that I was in a jungle, and that jungle must be in Vietnam. I sensed that I was in some way reliving my friend Dan's experiences in Vietnam.

I awoke to watch the ceiling moving above me as I was wheeled down a hallway and through a doorway labeled Radiology Department. I was moved onto a cold slab, and the X-ray machine was set to shoot images of my chest area and spine. The examination of the chest area was performed, and the radiologist noted that my heart appeared to be normal in size and configuration (an important conclusion, since the clinical diagnosis had indicated respiratory arrest). The lungs were clear of any active infiltration or consolidation (another important factor considering my history of asthma). The radiologist reached the conclusion "negative study," which meant that there were no physical abnormalities of the heart. He concluded that no gross fracture or displacement of the cervical spine (the vertebrae in my neck) could be identified.

I had apparently complained about back pains while in a semiconscious state. During the incident I had stumbled down a staircase and then fallen hard to the sidewalk, so the doctors had good reason to check for fractures. I had a throbbing and excruciating pain that ran through my spine from the base to my head, and I knew what had caused it. The pain was not caused by the fall, but by the reuniting of my spiritual being with my physical body when I was resuscitated in the ambulance. However, I certainly was not going to try to explain to the doctors that the pain was created by my soul's traumatic response to being imprisoned once again in a human body.

My dreams of being in the jungles of Vietnam continued in vivid color. I sensed I was actually there in another dimension of time and space. I felt the loneliness of the place, an acute need to survive at all costs, and a deep desire to return home. I could feel the overbearing heat and humidity; I could sense and smell the jungle. Suddenly, I sensed danger, followed by a blinding explosion of light and heat. Then I heard Dan's voice: *"It wasn't supposed to be this way! . . . This wasn't supposed to happen to me!"*

I awoke abruptly, startled. I was sweating profusely, my heart pounding. I could feel surges of adrenaline being secreted into my system. Rattled by the vivid dreams, and panicked that I was having another attack, I summoned the nurse with the call button. I had been lying in the darkened room for two days, and the searing pain that ran from the base of my spine to my neck had become even more acute. My physician and his associates had not arrived at a diagnosis, but I sensed somehow that they were withholding information from me.

I was correct in my assumption that information was being withheld. The drug screening had come back negative, so they reordered the testing, not believing that the first tests were accurate. The drug screening for cocaine was also negative, which must have surprised the doctors since a positive cocaine report would have supported the secondary admitting diagnosis of drug overdose. It would also have provided an explanation for the cause of the primary diagnosis of respiratory arrest. The doctors' focus on treating me as a drug overdose hung on the alleged report of a friend that I had been high on cocaine for two days. As it turned out, the basis for that claim had been an irresponsible and groundless comment made by a policeman at the scene.

The tests had shown alcohol in my system. The report registered an alcohol/blood level of 135 mg/dl, which meant that by clinical diagnosis I was legally intoxicated, but not to a degree that could have diminished my mental or motor faculties sufficiently to explain what had happened. An alcohol/blood level of 100-150 mg/dl constitutes a legally intoxicated state that would result in "euphoria, a disappearance of inhibitions, and a prolonged reaction time." A 150-200 mg/dl of alcoholic intoxication indicates "moderately severe poisoning, impaired reaction time, greatly prolonged loss of inhibition, and slight disturbances of equilibrium and coordination." A 200-250 mg/dl level of intoxication indicates a "severe degree of poisoning, disturbances of equilibrium and coordination, retardation of the thought processes and clouding of consciousness." The upper levels of alcoholic intoxication, 250-400 mg/dl, indicate a "deep, possibly fatal coma."

My alcohol/blood level of 135 was consistent with my report to the doctors that I had consumed several glasses of champagne. I had been drinking almost daily for twenty years, and being mildly intoxicated was a normal state of existence for me. I had developed a high tolerance for drinking; it was an occupational hazard for a nightclub owner. Since my alcoholic consumption prior to my collapse had been minimal, I also had to discount my drinking as a cause of my death visions.

The nurse, responding to the call button, came into my room.

"Yes, Mr. Dougherty, what can I do for you?"

My heart was pounding in my chest. I was irritated and upset, and rattled by the vivid dreams.

"I need something for this pain! Why am I being denied treatment?"

It must have seemed obvious to her that I was looking to be sedated with painkillers. In fact, I really would have liked a chilled bottle of Dom Perignon. "Your admitting diagnosis was for a drug overdose. Your doctor specifically requested no sedation."

"The toxicology reports came in this afternoon. There was no cocaine or any other drugs in my system," I responded angrily. "I've been trying to tell everyone in this damn hospital that I didn't take any drugs. No one seems to listen to me. Get my doctor on the phone right now. I want something for this back pain, and I want it now."

"It's the July Fourth holiday. I doubt that we can reach your doctor."

"Don't tell me you can't reach him. I want him beeped now and tell him I want something for this pain. If I don't get some consideration around here, I'm going to call my lawyers and sue this place," I fired back at her.

I was back into being my old self, expecting and demanding whatever I wanted. I was back in my old real world. The nurse left the door ajar, and I heard her shoes hitting the floor as she sprinted down the hall in a panic. The last thing a night nurse wanted on her floor was a screaming patient who would disturb the other patients and start a chain of unpleasant events.

I knew that the night nurse would have to inform my physician of my legal threat to sue the hospital and my request for sedatives. After all, now that it had been determined that I was not on illegal drugs, I thought that it would be sensible to put me on legal drugs. What I couldn't figure out was how I knew that they had already received the negative report on the drug screening that day, but failed to disclose that information to me.

Fifteen minutes went by before the telephone rang at the nurse's station. I knew it would be my physician on the other end. "Yes, Doctor, I'm sorry to bother you, but Mr. Dougherty has gotten very agitated and upset. . . . Yes, Doctor. . . . I know, Doctor . . . but we have a "no sedation" order. . . . The patient told me he knows the toxicology report came back negative. . . . Yes, Doctor, all right. . . . Cancel "no sedation" order. . . . Valium . . . 10 milligrams. . . . Good night, Doctor." She hung up the telephone.

Home run! I had correctly intuited that the negative toxicology report had been received. Valium wasn't my favorite cocktail, but under the circumstances, it was better than nothing at all. The nurse returned to my room and I got ten milligrams of Valium intravenously. As the sedative circulated through my blood system, the searing back pain began to subside, and I found myself levitating off the bed and floating away in soft white clouds.

It was Wednesday night, the Fourth of July, and a big night at Marakesh. Red, white, and blue bunting and American flags would decorate the club along with dozens of red, white, and blue balloons and patriotically designed fresh flower arrangements. The disc jockeys would spin disco versions of America's favorite patriotic songs. The champagne would flow, and so would the cocaine. A long line of patrons would be queuing at the club's entrance. VIPs, whose names were on the reservation list, would bypass the other patrons waiting in line and glide past the velvet ropes and stanchions into the club. The energy level at Marakesh on the Fourth of July was always at its highest level.

I had never missed a Fourth of July celebration at Marakesh, so I was initially depressed, but the Valium was improving my mood. The searing pain had disappeared. I resigned myself to the idea that I would be spending the evening alone, but floating on a drug-induced cloud relieved my aloneness. Suddenly, I felt an angelic presence enter the room. At first I thought that I was actually being visited by an angel, and I was, but it was an earthly angel, my new girlfriend, who had sneaked into my private room after visiting hours. She surprised me with a bottle of champagne, and we proceeded to have a party. After several glasses, she began to massage my sore and aching body.

After lying in the hospital for three days, my physical healing process was finally underway. The Valium masked the pain; the champagne answered the call of my craving for alcohol; and the massage made me feel human again. Suddenly, I was jolted from my dream-like state by a beam of light piercing into the darkened room from the doorway.

I looked toward the door and was startled by an ominous and darkly-clothed figure filling it. The beam of light radiated from the dark figure directly into my eyes. It hypnotized me, and I felt as if I was rising from the bed, drawn to the light.

The dark figure spoke to me in a deep voice that boomed out from behind the radiant light, "Ned Dougherty!"

"Yes," I responded meekly as I sat up, still drawn to the light.

"Are you Ned Dougherty?" the dark figure questioned, as I sensed the light coming closer.

"Yes, I'm Ned Dougherty." I was convinced that the dark figure was a spirit, and that I was being called back to the light by the spirit. I was now focused on making the transition, unaware and unconcerned with the physical world. I was going back to the Other Side, to the spiritual realms. I knew that the spiritual beings would not let me down, that my experience of death was an orientation program, and now they were coming back for me.

As the bright light came closer, I prepared to leave my body behind and proceed on my next journey. The dark being, now very close—right in front of me—spoke again. "I understand that you came very close to meeting God the other night."

"Actually, I did meet Him," I responded confidently. "I assume that you are here to bring me back?"

"Well, hopefully I can," he responded. But something was wrong here. The voice seemed too earthly.

I watched as the beam of light suddenly turned upward. I could now see the face and the piercing eyes of my visitor. He was wearing a black suit of clothing like the Angel of Death. Below his face, I recognized the Roman collar of a Catholic priest, and he was carrying a penlight that was now pointed upwards, revealing his much too earthly face. The beam of light came from his flashlight; it was obviously not "the light."

His voice became even more earthbound as he continued, "I saw you in the ICU the other night and administered last rites. I understand that they lost you in the ambulance for some time before the EMTs resuscitated you. Not many people get that close to God and live to tell about it."

I was disappointed by my visitor, and he sensed my disappointment. "Is there anything I can do for you? Were you expecting someone else tonight?"

"Well, actually I was. I was expecting someone else." It was all I could think to say as I became more sober and focused on the real world while floating on a drug-induced cloud of Valium and champagne.

"Well, let me know," he said as he retreated. "Let me know if there is anything I can do for you." He hesitated as if he had forgotten something. Then he proceeded to say a short prayer and give me his blessing, and then he was gone.

Startled back into reality, I collapsed onto the bed and stared at the ceiling. I thought I might be losing my mind. I actually believed I was being called back to the spiritual realms. It was a false alarm, but it would turn out to be the first of several.

My girlfriend came up from her hiding place. She had had the presence of mind to duck behind the bed when the door opened. I had forgotten that she was even there. We continued our party and drank the rest of the champagne.

She continued the massage, and I began to slip more comfortably into my body. As I allowed myself to fall into a pillow of clouds, I realized for the first time that my perception of reality was never going to be the same as it had been before my experience with death. My life and my perception of life had been changed forever. I knew I was a spiritual being in essence, but I was now a spiritual being enclosed in a human body. Therefore, I had human needs and human desires. I looked up and out the window into the night sky, up past planet Earth and out into deep space. I tried to focus my eyes far away into the universe. Several nights before, I had visited that place deep in space, but I had visited there in a different form, in a different dimension. The journey seemed so simple then; now it was impossible.

CHAPTER 13

GOING HOME

July 6, 1984

He who dies with the most toys is in for a big surprise!
—*Ned Dougherty*

I spent the first several days home from the hospital in peaceful contemplation. During the sunny days, I rested on a chaise lounge by the pool. Since leaving the hospital, I constantly marveled at the brightness the world seemed to have. I could stare into the pool and be mesmerized by the patterns made by breezes blowing across the water. I could gaze at a single drop of water on my fingertip, enthralled. I would focus on a tree, a shrub, or a flower and recognize the life force that emanated from each. I saw the world from a new perspective—as being part of God's creation.

I went shopping. I bought outdoor chimes and hung them in the garden that surrounded my pool. At night I lay on the chaise lounge staring up at the stars. The gentle breezes moved the chimes; their tinkling was reminiscent of the sounds I had heard during my experience. I sat outside all night long, waiting and wondering. I listened to the wind chimes for hours, comforted and relaxed by their strange new music. I was searching for something in this music, obsessed with searching for particular sounds, but I couldn't figure out what I was trying to hear or achieve.

It seemed as if I was being drawn to certain things, sounds, directions, people. This concept of being "drawn to" is difficult to explain. It was like having a powerful inner voice directing me in certain ways; maybe the spirits were still communicating with me on a sub-conscious level. For example, I was drawn to purchase a video called *Koyaanisqatsi* which turned out to be a visual story accompanied by music based on the tribal legends of the Hopi. The title was a Hopi Indian word meaning crazy life, life in turmoil, life disintegrating, life out of balance, a state of life that calls for another way of living.

I had to stay away from the nightclub for a while as I recuperated. Even the thought of going back to the noise and confusion of the night scene was unsettling. I preferred to remain at home listening to the soothing sounds of ethereal music, or preferably, to silence. I had much to think about before I got on with my life.

The last visit I had with my physician before being discharged from the hospital did not give me the answers I wanted. I knew I had been dead, and I knew that I had come back from death, but I could not discuss what I had experienced with the doctor. I was sure he would think that I was crazy. Despite my physical condition and lack of vital signs during this episode, none of the hospital tests resulted in a diagnosis that could sufficiently explain the physiological cause of what I experienced. Of greater concern to me was the experience itself. I had not been able to discuss it with anyone. It was consuming all of my time as I reviewed and analyzed every event in it. I was trying to live in two different realities, trying to reconnect with terra firma and trying to reach into the other side of existence. It was unsettling. One thing I knew for sure: I was alive and apparently healthy. As I learned during my death, I was being given a second chance in life.

I found myself reflecting on my life, particularly on my early childhood and teenage years, a time I had previously blocked out of my memory. I felt drawn to revisit my boyhood home in Hazleton. I especially wanted to visit the street in front of my grandmother's home I had visited during the experience. I had not been back to Hazleton in the ten years since my father's death in 1974, and I hadn't thought I would ever want to go back again. However, if the visions I had been shown of my future life were real, it meant that I was going to return to living in Pennsylvania at some point. As a matter of fact, I was sure that the mountainside and valley vision that I had been shown was actually located a short distance outside of Hazleton in an area called "Sugarloaf."

Sometime during the year prior to my near-death episode, I had received a phone call from a high school classmate reminding me that, as senior class president, it was my responsibility to organize the twenty-year class reunion. I was short, abrupt, and to the point with him. I had no interest in organizing a class reunion or spending a weekend with former classmates whom I had not seen in twenty years and didn't care if I ever saw again.

Now I was feeling differently about that class reunion, but it seemed as if it was already too late. I wanted to make amends to this classmate whom I had treated so rudely, but I didn't know how to get in touch with him or how to organize a reunion in Hazleton. Class reunions, especially after twenty years, took lots of planning, and I had lost contact with everyone from my class.

I decided to try to invite my classmates to the Hamptons and hold a class reunion at Marakesh. The high school had been closed for years, so I called the Hazleton Chamber of Commerce to see if they had any suggestions on how I could reach fellow classmates with the idea of publicizing such a class reunion. Ironically, I found myself talking to John Quigley, a younger graduate from St. Gabriel's. He was helpful in suggesting how I could promote the class reunion, but we spent most of the time talking about how things had changed in Hazleton.

Quigley had the unenviable responsibility of trying to revitalize the sagging downtown area of Hazleton by encouraging new businesses. Like many small cities in the United States, Hazleton was experiencing the flight of businesses to strip malls and indoor shopping centers located on the outskirts of the city, offering improved access roads and free parking. As small, locally owned businesses were closing in the downtown area, they were being replaced in the malls by national chains with managers, not local owners.

I related my particularly fond memories of Broad Street in Hazleton to Quigley. In the late 1950s, when I was in my early teens, I would walk with my friends around Broad Street, visiting the different soda fountains and flirting with the girls. We would stand in front of the Leader Store wearing khaki pants and penny loafers, whistling as the girls walked by. As we got older, we would ride around the block in one of the parents' cars, whistling at the girls. If you weren't driving your dad's car, you jostled and fought with your friends to ride "shotgun" in the front seat. It was like being in limbo to be stuck in the back seat, especially in two-door cars.

Downtown Broad Street was the center of our teen social life. We even had a dance club where, like Dick Clark's *American Bandstand*, the owner spun popular 45-rpm records. The Broad Street area was where everyone met—in the stores, on the street, at the soda fountains. Broad Street had two first-rate movie theaters, the Grand and the Capitol, and around the corner on Wyoming Street, the Feeley Theater offered westerns all Saturday for only a dollar. Parades, pep rallies, and street fairs were held on Broad Street in the 1950s and early 1960s. There were no drugs, violence, or crime then and the world seemed like a perfect place to live, at least from where we walked on Broad Street.

However, according to Quigley, the town I grew up in, and left in 1964, was no longer the same. I concluded that the area's young people had become exposed to acid rock, MTV, and an influx of drugs and crime. It was inconceivable to me that the problems of big cities would ever reach places like Hazleton. In addition to trying to revitalize downtown, Quigley was working with the youth of Hazleton.

I switched my attention from the class reunion for the moment and decided I wanted to do something to help Quigley and show my appreciation for the community that provided me with such fond memories. This was a brain shift for me; I actually felt inspired to do something good.

Quigley had mentioned that he was planning to kick off his campaign to revitalize downtown Hazleton by creating a special promotional event on Broad Street, but he lacked the resources to do it. I realized that I had all the resources available to do a street show. I had recently added a new dimension to Marakesh by introducing theatrical themes. I had hired a cast of actors, mostly college students majoring in performing arts, to create fantasy productions. In fact, we had recently created a live performance of Michael Jackson's "Thriller" video at the club. We had an actor named MJ who impersonated Michael Jackson, and an off-Broadway dance troupe that reproduced the "Thriller" video dance scenes.

I called Quigley back and offered to do the show at my expense. I had two conditions: I wanted the publicity to be directed to children and teenagers; the show was to be for them. I also wanted the theme of the show to be "Say No To Drugs!" Quigley excitedly accepted, but we had to move quickly. The kick-off campaign was only nine days away.

I arranged for two motor homes and a limousine to transport our theatrical troupe to Hazleton. They arrived the night before the show, which was publicized by the Chamber of Commerce. I flew up to Hazleton by helicopter, which we used to circle over Broad Street to videotape the show. When we arrived on Broad Street on Tuesday, July 17, at noon, we were surprised to find several thousand children and adults already waiting for the show to start. They surrounded a large flatbed trailer truck that had been set up in the middle of Broad Street with a large speaker system. The show was being broadcast live by the local radio station.

As our Michael Jackson impersonator walked onto the stage and led off the show by lip-synching the song, "Billie Jean," the kids went wild and cheered excitedly. To the crowd of younger children, MJ was the authentic Michael Jackson, as he sang and danced up and down the stage, dressed in white military pants, a blue military shirt with gold epaulets at the shoulders, and Michael Jackson's trademark single white glove and black sunglasses. As the sound system boomed out "Pretty Young Thing," the dance troupe joined MJ on the stage. Then, while MJ disappeared off the stage to change into his "Thriller" costume, the radio station interviewed me. During the interview, I thanked the people of Hazleton for the great turnout, and I told them how much I appreciated growing up in their great city. I said that the most important message of the day was "Say No To Drugs!"

When MJ returned to the stage in a red and black costume, he performed his rendition of "Thriller" with the dance troupe dressed as ghouls in white, black, and gray shredded and torn costumes. Their macabre-like faces were painted with gruesome green and yellow makeup. While the dance troupe performed their break-dancing routines, other members of the cast danced through the crowds, who were applauding and cheering loudly. The show was an enormous success. I was energized by the experience, and I thought to myself, *Several weeks ago, I never would have done something like this. I have been inspired to do something nice and wonderful by producing this show, and I feel very good inside because I have done something nice for other people.*

As I pondered these thoughts, I found myself walking around the crowd to a quieter corner of the street away from the crowd. For the first time, I noticed with sadness the facades of the storefronts. Many of the stores were closed or had signs posted: "Out of Business," "For Rent," or "Going Out of Business." I somehow knew that although our show to kick off the revitalization of downtown Hazleton was a success, Broad Street would never again be the same.

I leaned back against a building, listening to the loud music and the roar of the crowd. It was exhilarating. I looked up into the bright and cloudless sky at the helicopter hovering over the street. My friend Bill was hanging out the helicopter's doorway by a harness, videotaping the show below. The whirling blades of the helicopter momentarily hypnotized me. It was quite hot in the midday sun, and I started feeling strange. It wasn't just the heat from the sun; it seemed as if a heat was building up inside me. Suddenly, it seemed as if the heat source just burst through the top of my head, and a brilliant flash of light blinded me. As I began to refocus my eyes, I was still staring up at the whirling blades of the helicopter, but it was the incredible sight above and beyond the whirling blades that stunned me.

Across the panorama of the sky, I was startled by the ethereal image of the amphitheater and the thousands of spiritual beings in attendance. Set against the deep blue sky, the magnificent image appeared almost mist-like. I was so stunned that the image first appeared to be stationary like a still life. But then the panoramic view of the amphitheater became animated, and the thousands of spirits were cheering and applauding like the crowds in the street.

I must be hallucinating, I thought. I had not been drinking since I left the hospital, so I was sober, but I was taking Valium; perhaps this was a hallucination, an undesirable side effect of the Valium. I was sweating heavily, obviously in reaction to the midday sun. I realized that my heart had been pounding wildly, surges of adrenaline created painful tremors below my heart, and my breathing had become labored. But the vision in the sky did not disappear while I was going through the process of rationalizing these events.

An ambulance and crew of EMTs had been assigned to the show. I spotted them across the street, but as I tried to walk toward them I became faint and dizzy. The attendants saw me coming toward them and recognized that I needed help. I stumbled, almost collapsed, but managed to sit in the doorway of the ambulance. I asked them for some oxygen and explained to them that I was overcome by the heat and needed to rest for a while. While the EMTs checked my vital signs, I breathed deeply through the oxygen mask and began to relax. As I regained a more rhythmic pattern of breathing, the pounding of my heart began to subside. Finally, I regained control of myself and gathered the courage to look back up in the sky past the whirling blades of the helicopter. For me, it was a moment of recognition and acceptance. I could still see the spiritual beings arrayed in the amphitheater across the sky. I realized that I was the only one who could see them. My eyes were fixed on the sky while everyone else was enthralled with the street show.

The spiritual beings were gathered to watch the scenes below them and I remembered their message as it was repeated to me from the amphitheater when I had been "dead": "You are doing wonderfully. We are here to support you. You are part of us, and we are part of you. We stand ready to come to your aid when you need us, and you will. Call us. Beckon us. We will flock to you when the time comes."

I realized that we embodied humans are never alone. I now knew that the afterlife, which I had experienced, was a heavenly place of loving and compassionate spiritual beings and angels, beings who were among us and around us. I also knew that the angels and spiritual beings were working to inspire, protect, and guide us to recognize and perform our mission in life. As I continued to rest, I felt as if I was cycling down from the altered state of consciousness that had permitted me a glimpse of the spirit world. I began to realize that the physical symptoms that I had just experienced were the physical manifestation of a spiritual process that was taking place within my being, a process that enabled me to briefly glimpse a more ethereal state of reality, but definitely a reality.

I felt sufficiently calmed from this episode to thank the EMTs for their assistance and return to the show. The sky was again deep blue, but white clouds were gathering. The heavenly amphitheater was no longer visible to me, but I was certain that the celestial audience was still in attendance.

As MJ staged his "Thriller" act and the ghouls were dancing up and down the stage eliciting the screams of frightened children, I realized how warped our contemporary perception of death and the afterlife had become. While the ghouls on the stage represented the popular conception of the physically dead, the spiritual beings in the amphitheater represented the reality of the spiritual beings that survived beyond physical death. The afterlife *in reality* was much different from what was being portrayed on the stage.

Halloween has become a celebration of the afterlife, complete with ghosts, ghouls, and goblins. Hollywood capitalized on that concept to create scary and macabre movies, so that anything related to the spiritual afterlife became a representation of horrible creatures and ghosts. How different from the negative perception humans had created is the spiritual reality that I had visited—the afterlife as a positive place of joy, peace, and serenity.

I realized then that we would have to reinvent the "Thriller" show if we wanted to entertain children with an accurate portrayal of the positive side of the afterlife. We would have to present an uplifting spiritual show and fill people with joy, peace, and serenity if we were to portray the afterlife in a realistic way. I also realized that I was going to have to be open to seeing spirits and angels at unexpected times. I would have to learn to avoid having anxiety attacks every time I became aware of a supernatural presence.

As MJ finished the show and jumped down from the stage, he was mobbed by the screaming children who were all trying to reach out to touch him. The crowd began to disperse, and the cast and crew were invited to a local restaurant to celebrate. At the end of the day, the cast and crew returned to the Hamptons, except for the video staff. On the following day, we shot video scenes at St. Gabriel's High School and Church, and in my old neighborhood. I had been shown during my near-death episode that my future life would involve my making a movie in my former neighborhood in Hazleton. By remaining behind with the video crew, I was consciously trying to recreate those spirit scenes, but I felt that something was not quite right. I was forcing these events to take place to fulfill the visions. Perhaps, I thought, the scenes that I had been shown during my experience were supposed to take place at another time in my future.

When I returned to the Hamptons, I was exhilarated by the response to our street show in Hazleton. I felt that I had been given a second chance in life to do some good things to make up for all the bad things in my past. I felt that part of my mission in life was to get the message across to children to "Say No To Drugs!" and the street shows could provide the attraction to draw children and teenagers to communicate that message.

At the party following the street show, I had begun to drink champagne because I felt that I needed something to calm me down. I was still human; I wanted to celebrate; and champagne was my favorite medicine. The Valium didn't seem right, but I was taking it anyway. At first, I failed to see the irony: I had been oblivious to my own alcohol and drug consumption, while I was working on a plan to save the world from drugs.

Several days after the Hazleton trip, I began to run out of energy. Although I was elated by having glimpsed the spirit world and had been given a new opportunity to change the direction of my life, I had not prepared myself for the aftershock of my death episode. Although I was full of altruistic and optimistic ideas, I was still stuck in my old life. I was organizing an anti-drug campaign, yet I was still involved in the nightclub business. My new life, whatever it was going to be, was filled with contradictions.

CHAPTER 14

THE TWILIGHT ZONE

July-August 1984

> Our birth is but a sleep and a forgetting.
> The soul that rises with us, our life's star,
> Hath had elsewhere its setting,
> And cometh from afar:
> Not in entire forgetfulness,
> And not in utter nakedness,
> But trailing clouds of glory do we come
> From God, who is our home!
> —William Wordsworth

For the previous twenty days I had been trying to function normally, as if nothing had happened, but I couldn't. I was living in two different states of reality. The reality I was most familiar with was my Earth life. The other reality I had mostly forgotten since birth, but it was infinitely older than my Earth life; it was my spiritual life from before birth.

I had heard of birth described as a sleep and a forgetting. The problem for me was that I was now clearly aware of my spiritual origin, but I had difficulty trying to incorporate it into my new Earthly existence. As a newborn in 1946, I had the gift of forgetting my spiritual life before my birth, to enable me to discover my new world as a human being. Now my death-like return journey took the forgetting away, and I had to experience my earthbound reality as well as the Other Side. And I was not doing well at living in either world.

During my waking hours, I was trying to recover physically and function normally. I threw myself back into my business interests, organizing and promoting events at the nightclub. During the night, I kept re-experiencing the events of my "death." I had periods of peace and contentment when I focused on the loving, caring, and understanding that I had been shown while in the light. Then I would awaken from my sleep, heart palpitating, sweating, and trembling, after dreaming about the prophesied Earth changes that I had seen during my death journey.

I also awoke with nightmares of being in Vietnam. These dreams were so vivid that I almost felt as if I had been teleported to Vietnam at the time when the events I dreamed had taken place. I began to realize that Dan McCampbell was still with me in my dreams, and that I was being shown the actual events that took place during his final days in Vietnam.

Day and night following the hospitalization, I had to attempt to deal with living in different realities. I was continually processing the experience in my mind while trying to conduct day-to-day business affairs. I did have one advantage. I would be in a conversation with someone and would finish their sentence for them or respond before they were finished talking to me. I seemed to have retained the mental telepathy I experienced in my near-death state. I recognized that people had fields of energy or auras emanating from them. I watched how a person's aura would change depending on the environment or because of different people around them. I saw that one person's thoughts and actions would also affect another person's aura.

I could sense people's reactions to me, so I knew what they thought of me despite what they said. I saw some people whose auras were constantly dark or cloudy, as if they carried a storm over their heads. Others constantly walked in the light with a brilliant golden or bright white aura about them. How wonderful it would be if every human could communicate telepathically and read the auras of those around them. In such a perfect world, there would be no chance for lying or deception because every person's true thoughts, feelings, and emotions would always be readable in their aura. Those people who chose to be negative and deceptive would wear their true nature like a uniform. On the other hand, those who chose to live positively and honestly would recognize each other and would be drawn to each other's light.

During my "death" experience, I had been told that humankind would evolve into a new and more spiritually transformed race of beings. Perhaps it was part of God's plan to give humankind these gifts. Then people could recognize their own positive or negative states as well as the positive or negative states of other people on the basis of the aura. Perhaps God would bestow upon mankind the ability to communicate telepathically, so that human beings could only then communicate honestly with each other. I tried to imagine what the world would be like if it were free of the diseases of misunderstanding and deception. I realized what it would be like; it would be like the world of spirit—like heaven.

Realizing I had the gifts of communicating telepathically and reading auras led to another revelation. I sensed that if I focused on certain individuals, I could not only read their aura, I could also envision negative events that were to take place in their lives. I felt that in some cases I could do something to alter these events. I began to make a mental list of people who I felt needed my assistance and made plans for how I was going to come to their assistance. I was developing lists and plans that I could not discuss with anyone. It was a tremendous amount of activity taking place at the same time. The sensory overload was such that I thought my brain was going to fry.

One afternoon, twenty days after my hospitalization, I was driving on the same road that the ambulance had taken on July 2. My girlfriend was sitting next to me. She had been with me since I was released from the hospital and was assisting me with the nightclub shows. While I was driving, I was also mentally integrating my normal human activities with the agenda I received during my near-death experience. I was planning a St. Gabriel's High School reunion prom to be held at Club Marakesh. I was working on organizing the anti-drug street-show campaign. I had to learn about the film industry since I was going to become involved in making films, so I was making inquiries about film school courses for the fall semester. I was going over my list of friends who I believed (according to my psychic insights) were going to need my assistance. I contacted real estate brokers in the geographical area that contained the valley and mountainside that I saw during my experience to find out if the property was for sale. I did not previously intend to buy property in that area, but I now knew that I would eventually; I had no other choice.

I had to start writing soon, but I did not know what I was going to write. I had to start working on an outline to conduct a seminar at a university, but I did not know what I was going to say. I had to get ready to travel extensively, but I didn't know my travel agenda. I had to try to save the world from wars, violence, drugs, earthquakes, hurricanes, floods, and fires, but didn't know how I was going to proceed. In effect, I was trying to plan immediately for every future vision that I had been shown.

Driving down the highway, I felt I was going to implode from thought overload. Suddenly a brilliant flash of light went through me, and I was immediately relieved of all those plans and thoughts. I felt relieved for the first time in many days. Defensively, I began to think that maybe this had all been a dream, that the death experience had never happened, that I didn't have this new mission in life, that maybe this was all just a hallucination. I finally decided *Yes, that is the case!* Now I could go back to my old life. This was just a bad drug trip. However, I was not on drugs. Or was I? What about the Valium? More confusion.

Closer to the village, we passed the entrance to the airport, which was also an Air National Guard facility. As I drove past the airport entrance doing about 60 miles per hour, I noticed a hitchhiker in military fatigues. Although I was moving fast, I found myself focusing directly upon his face, and I thought I recognized his engaging smile. I could have sworn it was Dan. I focused on him in my rearview mirror. As I did, I began to drift into the oncoming traffic and avoided an accident only by swerving to the right; then I slammed on the brakes and stopped. I jumped out of the car, but the hitchhiker was gone. I could not explain my bizarre behavior to my girlfriend. However, I had enough sense to ask her to drive us home, which we did in silence. I needed a drink. It was my medicine of choice—the only way to deal with my fear that people would think I was going crazy.

Later that evening, I found myself drinking heavily at Marakesh and using Valium. I left the club alone and visited another bar where I continued to drink alone. As I left the bar, I lost consciousness and collapsed in a parking lot. I was picked up by the ambulance, rushed to the hospital, and admitted into the emergency room in a comatose state. Again. The same tests were conducted. The echocardiogram for mitral prolapse was negative; the CAT scan was negative; the X-rays were negative; the drug test was negative.

I did not have any out-of-body experiences; nor did I see spiritual beings or go through a tunnel of light. Trying to deal with the enormity of the recent events in my life, I just drank until I passed out. My blood alcohol level was dangerously high, 214 mg/dl, and combined with the prescribed Valium, this episode could have been fatal.

After five days, I was sent home from the hospital with another prescription for Valium. During the next two weeks, I passed out on two separate occasions while having dinner in restaurants. Both times I was taken by ambulance to the hospital, but the process had become so routine that I refused admission and returned to my home.

In addition to my attempts to deal with the death episode, I was aware that I had a physical problem that was causing these blackouts. I decided to quit the Valium, assuming that it was the source of the blackouts, but the episodes continued. Although the blackouts would always follow my drinking, there was no reason for me to suspect that my drinking was the source of the problem. I was in denial, and I didn't know it.

Since I was not getting satisfactory answers as to what was wrong with me physically, I decided that I would be more successful in my medical treatment if I went to a major medical center. I chose Duke University Medical Center in Durham, North Carolina, because of its outstanding reputation. Even so, this was a curious decision. Even though I had never spent any time in North Carolina, I was somehow drawn there, and specifically to Duke Medical Center. North Carolina was a location that for some reason would figure significantly in my future. But when? And for what reason? Was I again trying to fulfill a prophetic vision of my future by going to North Carolina, or was I being drawn there in search of answers along my spiritual journey? Although I could not logically explain the decision to go to North Carolina, even to myself, I knew I was being drawn there and I uncharacteristically made the decision to go.

On Sunday evening, August 12, I landed at Raleigh-Durham Airport. The air was so hot, muggy, and still that you could cut it with a knife. During the night I slept restlessly, questioning why I had found it necessary to come here. A staff doctor had set up a three-day schedule of tests and procedures to determine the cause of my blackouts. So I spent three days traveling through the maze of buildings and departments getting every kind of test, only to learn that I would have to wait to get all the results. I returned to New York, but decided I would come back to Duke after the summer season was over in the Hamptons. I had a sense that I was being drawn back to North Carolina.

I could have returned to the Hamptons and sought medical attention at one of several major hospitals a short distance away in the New York City area, but I was looking for more than solutions to my medical problems, and for some reason I believed that in North Carolina I would find the answers to what concerned me most—my spiritual experiences. I was living silently with the belief that no one else could possibly have experienced what I had experienced on the night of July 2. I could not reach out to anyone and share what I had experienced.

Little did I know at the time that many other people had had "death" experiences very similar to mine. Although several medical doctors, scientists, and researchers were already investigating this phenomenon, it would be years before the public would become aware of this kind of experience. It was 1984, and I was totally in the dark. However, I was inspired to believe that I would become enlightened when I returned to Duke in the fall.

CHAPTER 15

THE WALL

September 1984

There is an appointed time for everything,
and a time for every affair under the heavens.
A time to be born, and a time to die;
a time to plant, and a time to uproot the plant.
A time to kill, and a time to heal;
a time to tear down and a time to build.
A time to weep, and a time to laugh;
a time to mourn, and a time to dance.
A time to scatter stones, and a time to gather
them;
a time to embrace, and a time to be far from
embraces.
A time to seek, and a time to lose;
a time to keep, and a time to cast away.
A time to rend, and a time to sew;
a time to be silent, and a time to speak.
A time to love, and a time to hate;
a time of war, and a time of peace.

Ecclesiastes 3:1–8

I spent the rest of the summer in the Hamptons trying to balance my recovery with my business activities. My blackout episodes ceased, but I was still extremely fatigued, and I was looking forward to returning to Duke. I was intrigued by the possibility that I would find answers to my spiritual journey by returning to North Carolina.

I celebrated my thirty-eighth birthday alone by taking the train to Washington, D.C., for a weekend stay before flying to Durham and Duke for further tests. I was also drawn to Washington because of an intense desire to visit the Vietnam War Memorial, an agenda item I had been contemplating since July 2.

I felt that by visiting the memorial I would somehow reconnect with my friend Dan. As a matter of fact, I believed that he was somehow influencing me from the Other Side to make this trip. I was also intrigued by the future visions that seemed to indicate that Washington would become a significant place for me at some point in the future; but I did not understand for what purpose I would become involved in politics or government. However, I did recognize that by going to Pennsylvania, Washington, and North Carolina I was being "drawn" to places that figured significantly in my future.

I arrived in Washington on Thursday morning and took a cab from Union Station to the Watergate Hotel. I had returned from my death episode with an agenda that included a concern about the future course of the United States and a number of controversial issues in which I previously had no interest. I began to make inquiries at a number of government offices and think-tanks. I had to make a number of requests under the Freedom of Information Act since some of the information I was trying to obtain was not available to the public and was considered classified.

On Sunday morning, September 23, I walked briskly to the Washington Mall and the entrance to the Vietnam War Memorial. The streets of Washington were deserted, except for a few joggers and the homeless huddled in doorways or in cardboard boxes. There were very few pedestrians or cars. I approached a dimly-lit booth manned by a National Park Service ranger who provided information about the Vietnam War Memorial. I inquired about finding a particular name on the wall of the memorial.

I gave the ranger Dan's name. He flipped through a well-worn book that resembled a telephone directory, found the name, and wrote down the panel and line number. I briefly read the pamphlet that the park ranger provided along with directions on how to locate Dan's name. As I walked down the tree- and shrub-lined path, I was struck by the early dawn scene. Out of the darkness, the memorial appeared like a giant scar in the rolling lawn, now covered with dew. I realized why people call it "The Wall." The polished black granite jutted out of the ground, dark and ominous, dimly lit by recessed lights.

The 58,182 names of the dead and missing were inscribed on the wall chronologically from the beginning to the end of the war. I felt as if I were walking back into a period in history that ripped the nation's soul. The names of the dead seemed to rise out of the ground on the black granite slab. *All those names.* It seemed as if part of the spirit of each reached out from the wall to touch me as I walked by. I reached the center and looked up at the vertex rising ten feet out of the ground. I seemed to have journeyed into a valley of death, surrounded by the souls of over 58,000 humans whose lives had been cut short.

I continued along the wall to the end where the wall again rose out of the ground. I approached Dan's panel and counted the lines from the top before settling at his line, then moved my finger through the line to the name: Daniel McCampbell. I stepped back from the wall to focus on this one name among many. My eyes blurred, and I lost his name among the lines. There were so many names. My tears were causing the blurring. The polished black granite came alive. It seemed as if I had stepped into the wall and found myself re-experiencing the dreams of Vietnam. I watched in rapid sequence the events of Dan's last moments in Vietnam, followed by a bright flash of light. The wall was dark again, but I felt heartache well up inside me, and my tears flowed. I was feeling the loss of only one name on the wall, yet the grief was unbearable. Maybe I was grieving for the families and friends of all the humans killed in Vietnam.

Seventeen years after Dan's death, I was experiencing the sorrow of his loss as if it had just happened. I felt his family's loss. For Dan, it was not supposed to be this way; it was not supposed to happen like this; it was not supposed to end this way. He had dreams and visions of a life filled with love for his family. Dan loved life, and he loved the world.

The wall became a blur again as I stepped back from it. I had been standing in front of it for an hour and the darkness around me had turned into daylight. As I stepped away, Dan's name became less and less visible among the many names surrounding it. Each name on the wall stood for another story; another life whose dreams, hopes, and love had been dashed away by a war we still do not understand.

I was overwhelmed by the spiritual presence at the wall. I saw the images of thousands of soldiers seemingly waiting in the spiritual world for closure and healing. It seemed as if they were reaching out from beyond the veil of the mirrored granite surface to communicate with their loved ones. Each soul that passed on witnessed the heartache and the loss of their loved ones. They wanted to cross that veil that separated them from the physical world, to inspire the ones left behind. They appeared in dreams and visions, as inner voices or inspirations, or by reaching into the hearts of loved ones when they were in prayer or meditation.

At their moment of death, they journeyed from the battlefield and from the awful carnage and horror of the war. Instantly, they transported themselves in their new spiritual state back to their hometowns and homes, where they tried to communicate with the ones they loved. They saw their wives and children, mothers and fathers, brothers and sisters, and friends shortly after the moment of their transition through death. They watched as the doorbells rang, and the death notices were received. In spirit, some of them attended their own funerals.

And all the while, they attempted to contact those that they loved. Many of those mourning their loss would experience their presence, distinctly sensing that their fallen soldier was nearby, although they could not always hear or see them. Some of the survivors would hear inner or exterior voices of their loved ones trying to communicate with them. Many survivors experienced a feeling or a touch from an invisible hand, or even an invisible hug or a kiss or a caress, a fragrance or a scent. Many survivors had visual experiences of the one they loved. They appeared to their spouses in their homes, usually at the foot of their spouse's bed. They appeared to their children, usually in their bedrooms or outdoors in their playgrounds. They appeared as if in a fine mist and always looking beautiful, radiant, and healed.

When the deceased tried to reach out to their survivors, they were often accompanied by lights or lamps blinking on and off. Sometimes radios, televisions, or record players turned on automatically. At other times, pictures, photographs, or hanging objects would move, turn over, or simply jump off the wall. Many mourners would reach out for a sign and be instantly visited by a swarm of butterflies, a flock of birds, a rainbow, the blooming of a flower, or the caress of a pet. Instinctively, the survivors knew that their deceased loved ones were sending them a sign.

The deceased wanted those they had left behind to know that it was okay to cry, that they were okay, that life could go on, that they could move on, that everything would be all right, and that "we will meet again in heaven." They wanted their loved ones to know: "go on with your life. I will always be there for you. I love you. It's time to say goodbye. . . ."

I thought about my dad's death. I knew he had communicated to me shortly after his death when I was driving across Nebraska. From my own death episode, I knew that what I experienced with my dad was not a hallucination, but was real for me. In the same way, I also knew that the souls of those killed in Vietnam were inspiring those they had left behind, just as Dan had reached out to me. I knew how difficult it is for the departed to reach their loved ones. Many in mourning are consoled by these inspirations, but many are angry, bitter, fearful, or too confused to accept the messages. Many think they were having hallucinations, seeing things, or going crazy because they don't believe such communications were possible, or because they don't believe in an afterlife. I used to be that way; now I know differently.

CHAPTER 16

A RAY OF SUNSHINE

October 1984

On Children:
You may give them your love but not your thoughts,
For they have their own thoughts.
You may house their bodies but not their souls,
For their souls dwell in the house of tomorrow,
which you cannot visit, not even in your dreams.
—*Kahlil Gibran, The Prophet*

When I arrived at the Duke Medical Center following my weekend in Washington, I felt eighty years old and not in good shape. My muscles and bones ached all over. I was given a secondary diagnosis of malaise and fatigue by the Duke medical team. These symptoms would have been understandable for someone who had recently suffered a heart attack, which I thought was what had happened to me when I had first been hospitalized. I was experiencing many of the symptoms of patients who suffered such attacks, but there was a major difference in my case. The doctors at Duke could find no organic evidence to suggest cardiovascular, pulmonary, neurological, or other organic causes for what they now were labeling "stress-related syncopal episodes."

I had planned to stay at Duke for two months, hoping that it would be sufficient for my recovery. However, I was frustrated again by the lack of a clear diagnosis, one that was understandable and acceptable. I settled into a routine of visiting the health club while the doctors developed a course of treatment for me.

Thursday evening I was sitting alone in a Pizza Hut near Duke. It was the dinner hour, and the restaurant was crowded, mostly with people from the medical center and university. I was drawn to the jukebox, which was playing Michael Jackson's "Thriller." A young boy in a wheelchair was accompanied by a woman who I guessed was his mother. It was one of those moments when the increased awareness of my psychic capabilities became intense. I had become increasingly troubled by these experiences and wanted to ease them from my mind. I felt that this increased psychic activity was preventing me from resuming a normal life. I tried to refocus on eating the pizza and putting aside the vivid messages that I was receiving, perhaps from my friend Dan.

Unable to stop the images, I focused on the boy and his mother. I saw that the boy's father had served in the Marine Corps in Vietnam, and that he had been exposed to Agent Orange, an herbicide containing the toxic contaminant dioxin. Agent Orange had been applied to the jungle by aerial spraying, which had been extremely effective in killing all the vegetation. As a result of the father's exposure, the deadly chemicals in

Agent Orange were responsible for the boy's serious birth defects.

I had been aware of the controversy about Agent Orange and how it had affected the lives of many Vietnam veterans, but the issue had not previously been of any interest to me. I knew nothing about Agent Orange affecting the spouses and offspring of those who were directly exposed to the deadly chemicals in Vietnam. I now realized that this boy in the wheelchair was one of thousands of children who were born malformed because of a parent's exposure to Agent Orange.

While I continued to observe the young boy and his mother, I psychically perceived that the United States government, as a matter of policy, was attempting to thwart any investigations concerning Agent Orange. Our government was trying to deny the link between Agent Orange and the increasing and varied medical problems that were affecting veterans, their spouses, and their children. The government was more concerned with avoiding the scandal and potential liability than with accepting its responsibility to provide for its own people who were suffering from Agent Orange. I intuited that the greatest concern of the government was that a full investigation of Agent Orange would result in both civil and criminal penalties against the military and industrial entities and individuals responsible for its production and use. The spraying of Agent Orange in Vietnam would turn out to be one of the greatest human and ecological disasters of all time, and it was being covered up.

Before my death episode, I would have had no interest in Agent Orange or any other serious controversial subject. I was only interested in my own materialistic and hedonistic world. I would have avoided looking at anyone in a wheelchair, young or old. I was only attracted to what I perceived as "beautiful people." Now I had this new sense of awareness, fueled by a powerful force of intuition that seemed to be redirecting the attractions and activities of my life. I found myself taken with this boy in the wheelchair and his plight. I sensed he had a strong and determined spirit and that he accepted his difficulties. I sensed that he was an inspiration to his parents and loved ones for his ability to accept his difficulties with such a strong spirit.

Then I heard a distinct inner voice instruct me: "Go speak to this boy and his mother."

I walked to the jukebox, pretending to be interested in making a selection. As the boy in the wheelchair looked up at me and smiled, I seized the opportunity to introduce myself. "Hi! My name is Ned. What's yours?" I said, as I knelt beside his wheelchair.

"Hi! I'm Teddy," he replied. "Do you like Michael Jackson's music? I do! He's my favorite!" In his demeanor, Teddy appeared to be about fourteen years old, yet his body was that of a much younger boy. He was securely fastened to his wheelchair. Any physical movement was difficult for him. I acknowledged his mother with a smile. She seemed pleased that a stranger had shown an interest in speaking with her son.

"Sure, I like Michael Jackson's music. As a matter of fact, I'm in the nightclub business and we play his music all the time." I then told Teddy all about the "Thriller" shows that I produced at the club and the street show in Hazleton. He listened enthusiastically. I explained that we had a Michael Jackson impersonator who performed for us.

"Boy! I would sure like to see Michael Jackson someday!" he responded excitedly.

"Well, maybe I can arrange that for you, Teddy," I replied. "Let's see what we can do." Something had already clicked in my mind. I was inspired to do something good for Teddy.

As Teddy watched the flashing, multicolored lights on the jukebox, I stepped around it and introduced myself to his mother. She told me that she had brought Teddy to Duke Medical Center for testing prior to a serious operation that was about to be scheduled. It was to be one more of many operations that Teddy had to endure to attempt to correct the abnormalities of his body. I already noticed that Teddy's physical complications had not adversely affected his mind or spirit. He had a wonderful spirit for a young boy who had to endure so much pain. He was so strong in spirit, he seemed almost angelic. When I first noticed Teddy across the restaurant, his aura had attracted me: it filled the restaurant with its positiveness.

Teddy's mother told me her husband was a Marine sergeant and that they were living at the Marine Corps Air Station in Cherry Point, North Carolina. She mentioned how fortunate they were that her husband was in the Marines because they never would have been able to take care of Teddy due to the astronomical medical bills. Although Teddy's mother was obviously a strong and courageous woman, I sensed a momentary feeling of despair as she talked about the impending surgery. When Teddy's mother began to excuse herself and Teddy, indicating that they had to leave, I interrupted their departure.

"I know this may sound strange coming from a perfect stranger," I said cautiously, "but I may be able to do something for Teddy. I would appreciate it if you would allow me to contact you." Teddy's mother thought about my offer for a few seconds, then she told me how I could reach her husband at Cherry Point.

During the previous summer on one of my trips to Hazleton, certain events took place that enabled me to recognize how I could help bring the light of God into Teddy's life. While walking in my old Elm Street neighborhood, I met my boyhood friend, Joe Zogby, who was visiting with his mother. Joe, a Vietnam veteran, had a career position with the federal government in Atlanta, where he lived with his wife, Margie, and their two children. Joe and I had grown up together and were good friends, but we had lost touch with each other over the years. As kids we had built model railroads together, and we were railroad fans, hiking on the railroad tracks and chasing freight trains.

Joe and I decided to take a leisurely drive to the village where my grandparents' Stockton General Store and Post Office had been located. Now the spot was just another empty lot strewn with debris and overgrown brush. The town of Stockton had become like every other small coal-mining town after World War II, gradually dismantled and forgotten. As Joe and I walked around the deserted lot, I remembered the many summer days I had spent at Gram's store. I remembered the shrill of the train's whistle echoing up and down the valley as the steam locomotive, chugging loudly and hissing steam, slowed down on its way to Hazleton, leaving only a mail bag to prove to the unemployed miners that the rest of the world was still in existence.

This train had been the signal for the local miners' children to go to the post office for the mail. They hardly ever received any mail of interest. They usually walked back home disappointed, carrying an advertisement addressed to the occupant of a post office box; sometimes they carried a relief check. I had often wondered then why the Stockton children seldom wore pants or shoes that were not patched excessively. Now, as I remembered the sadness of their faces, I realized how fortunate I was.

After leaving Stockton, Joe and I drove north to Angela Park, an amusement park with a large swimming pool that Joe and I had frequented as youths. As we passed the entrance, a sign greeted us: "Welcome Sunshine Foundation!" Joe and I walked around the park and met an older man whom we both knew from our youth. He was Lenny Gibson, an energetic man in his sixties, who looked much younger, and emanated a vibrant energy when we greeted him. I soon recognized that it was the charitable work he did that invigorated him. Lenny explained that he was holding a benefit fund-raiser at the park, compliments of the park's owners, the Barletta family. Joe and I agreed to buy a block of tickets as a donation and to give the tickets away to some of the children who gathered around us.

Lenny insisted that we go on the Alpine Ride, a series of suspended gondola cars that traveled by high-tension wires from one pole structure to another from the entrance of the park to the swimming pool area and back. I traveled with Lenny in one of the gondola cars (Joe followed in another), and asked him to tell me about the Sunshine Foundation.

"The Sunshine Foundation grants the last wish of a child who is either terminally or critically ill. We raise the money to grant the wish of the child—no matter what it is. Sometimes we run benefits like this one at the park, and other times we just go door to door and ask for twenty-five-cent donations."

"And how did this all get started?" I asked.

"It all started with a policeman in Philadelphia by the name of Bill Sample. After being assigned duty at a hospital where he saw many terminally ill children, Bill decided he wanted to do something for them, so he started going door to door asking for twenty-five-cent donations."

I realized that the Sunshine Foundation was a worthy organization. I did not know why at the time, but I had a strong feeling that it was not a coincidence that Joe and I met Lenny Gibson in the park that day.

Lenny continued. "I had been visiting a child in a hospital as a hospice volunteer when a nurse gave me a pamphlet about the Sunshine Foundation. After I read it, I formed a local chapter. The child that I had been visiting wanted to go to Disney World. As soon as we raised enough donations, he got his wish!" Lenny radiated a positive energy, and I could sense the deep satisfaction he received from his charitable work.

"Most children want to go to Disney World," Lenny continued, "so now we own a condominium in Orlando, Florida, that is shared by sixteen chapters of the national organization. American Airlines provides the transportation free of charge, and the State of Florida provides police services to the families and their children."

Listening to Lenny, I saw how great charitable works could develop from the efforts of one individual. Bill Sample, acting alone, had started the Sunshine Foundation. As his goodwill and work continued, his idea developed into a national organization, an army of angels helping critically and terminally ill children.

When the Lady of Light had showed me visions of my future life, my future mission in life included the creation of an organization called Mission of Angels. It occurred to me that meeting Lenny Gibson and hearing about the work of the Sunshine Foundation was not just a coincidence. I learned from Lenny Gibson how I could make a difference in Teddy's young life and begin to perform the kind of good works that would eventually lead to the creation of the Mission of Angels Foundation.

The day after I met Teddy and his mother at the Pizza Hut, I began to make telephone calls. First, I called

Lenny Gibson in Hazleton and told him about Teddy, and Lenny and I discussed how to grant Teddy his wish. Next, I called the Jackson "Victory Tour" office. I knew that Michael and the Jacksons were currently on a national concert tour, and I was hoping for a concert date in North Carolina. I spoke with Ellen, a very cooperative assistant, and informed her of our plans. Unfortunately, when she read the itinerary of future concerts, none had been scheduled for North Carolina. That was disappointing news since any long distance travel would be difficult for Teddy.

However, my hopes brightened when she added excitedly, "The Jacksons' tour will be appearing in Atlanta on Saturday, only two weeks away." Atlanta was close enough. I arranged for special tickets for Teddy, his mother, and two escorts. I would accompany Teddy and his mother to Atlanta where Joe Zogby would escort us to the concert. Many organizations and people were involved in getting Teddy to the concert in Atlanta, yet few of the people involved in coordinating the trip would ever personally meet or get to know Teddy.

On Friday evening, I flew from Raleigh-Durham to Kinston, North Carolina, to prepare to escort Teddy and his mother to Atlanta the following morning. I checked in at a motel and went to a nearby restaurant-bar that was crowded with young Marines. I found a place at the bar and became engaged in conversation with some of the Marines. I immediately thought of Dan and believed that he was guiding me from the Other Side to perform this mission for Teddy. The Marines were polite and mannerly and addressed me as "Sir." I perceived that some of these Marines were from broken and dysfunctional homes and some of them were from good families; some had been juvenile delinquents and some were good students.

It was apparent to me that the discipline and training of the Marine Corps had a positive and motivational impact on their lives. How unfortunate that they had to be trained as fighting and killing machines. How unfortunate it was that we did not live in a world in which the military training and discipline that these men received could be used more directly for good by having them perform acts of peace and goodwill—without the chaos and violence of war. However, I recognized that such thoughts were idealistic and naive in our "real" world.

Saturday morning, I arrived at Teddy's home and met his father. During our conversation, Teddy's father talked about his career in the Marine Corps, mentioning his service in Vietnam. I asked if he had been exposed to Agent Orange while he was in Vietnam. He responded that he was not sure, but that they were "always spraying stuff that would fall on us and our equipment."

Teddy's parents had decided not to inform Teddy until that morning that he was going to the concert. Teddy's father sat with his son and informed him that he was going to Atlanta to see Michael Jackson in concert, just as he had wished. Teddy's father added, "Total strangers are out there doing this for you, arranging for you to go to the Michael Jackson concert. Everything is being paid for. It shows that there is a lot of good in the world. There hasn't been much good that has taken place in your life. This is one of the very few good things, so enjoy it. The good Lord's looking down on you."

Our flight landed in Atlanta several hours before the concert. Joe Zogby and his wife, Margie, who had arranged our transportation, accommodations, and tickets, met us. After we checked in at the hotel, we brought Teddy to the concert. We were ushered through a special VIP entrance by Michael Jackson's own security personnel. The concert had already started as we entered the stadium field. The security personnel took Teddy right up to the front of the stage to the VIP area, where he immediately became exhilarated by the sights and sounds. This experience was his dream come true.

CHAPTER 17

THE MYSTICAL PILL

November 1984

> Man cannot discover new oceans,
> until he has the courage to lose sight of the shore.
>
> —*Anonymous*

During my first few weeks at Duke I was frustrated by the lack of a clearly defined and understandable diagnosis. I wanted to hear a doctor say, "You did have a heart attack; you did die; and you were resuscitated. Now it's time to get on with your life." Such a diagnosis would end a lot of discussion. It would have explained much of what I had experienced. However, I would still have had to deal with the experience itself: hearing my heart stop beating, leaving my body, being greeted by Dan, the tunnel of energy, the embracing light, the life review, the spiritual beings, the return to my body.

I was not telling anyone about this experience. I kept remembering the admonishment of the nurse in the intensive care unit: "If you don't stop talking that nonsense, we are going to have to call the psychiatrist in here." My survival instincts told me to stop talking, and I was cautious not to mention anything about the experience to any medical professional.

However, shortly after I arrived at Duke, I requested psychiatric consultation. I was given an appointment with a psychiatrist who specialized in psychopharmacology, the branch of psychiatry that involves prescribing psychoactive drugs. After several sessions, he suggested an antidepressant medication to curb the "stress-related syncopal attacks." After years of experience in the nightclub and drug sub-culture and my negative experiences with Valium, I refused to medicate myself to avoid dealing with the issues present in my life. I wanted to work, not sleep through them. I did not want to mask or avoid them by taking drugs. I told this psychiatrist I was not interested in pills to cure my problems. I explained to him that drinking was my medicine of choice and that I would prefer to drink, not take pills, if I felt anxious. I guess they didn't have too many alcoholics in North Carolina because this psychiatrist should have recognized the symptoms.

The symptoms were obvious and clearly stated in my medical records: I was Irish Catholic, a member of an ethnic group with a high rate of alcoholism. My father was an alcoholic who had died from cirrhosis of the liver. I was a nightclub owner, a profession with a high rate of alcoholism. Furthermore, in each of the episodes various amounts of alcohol were present. Yet not one doctor considered the possibility that I may have had a drinking problem. I didn't bring it up because I couldn't imagine my life without drinking.

Since I was uncooperative in accepting medication, I was referred to the stress management and biofeedback department. If I wasn't inspired to avoid drugs, I could have readily gravitated to the psychopharmacological approach. My decision to avoid drug treatment was a significant turning point not only in my treatment, but also in the course of my life. I began regular biofeedback sessions. These consisted of sitting in a comfortable sofa chair while being monitored by the biofeedback machine, which was attached to contact points on my body to monitor heart rate and blood pressure. By being made aware of my responses, it was my task to attempt to alter and control muscle tension and blood flow to reduce anxiety. In other words, I had to learn how to relax.

I found it curious that the same department of psychiatry would alternately prescribe drugs and/or stress management and relaxation to supposedly achieve the same results. As a matter of fact, I became curious about the profession of psychiatry.

I heard that Sigmund Freud was a cocaine addict. I was a nightclub owner, and I knew all about cocaine. Sometimes my friends even referred to me as "the doctor." From what I knew about cocaine, it didn't surprise me that Freud was also obsessed with sex, finding sex as the drive behind practically any and all human behavior. In the nightclub and drug culture, everyone that I knew had both of these characteristics in common with Freud.

Meanwhile, it seemed to me there was a war within the profession. The psychopharmacologists, who reduced all mental or emotional disorders to a function of chemistry, seemed to be hell-bent on creating complex drugs to prescribe. The biofeedback and stress management teams seemed to be pursuing a holistic and even spiritual approach to working with their patients. At this point, I liked the latter approach.

One day I was given an appointment with a clinical psychologist. He surprised me with the Rorschach test, a series of inkblot cards supposedly designed to analyze a patient's emotional and intellectual functioning and integration. The psychologist asked me to view each card and give him a response as to how I was stimulated by each inkblot. My response to each of the ten cards was the same. I concluded that the designer of the Rorschach test had been on drugs to come up with the ink blot test. The creator of the test, it turns out, was a Swiss psychiatrist, Hermann Rorschach, who reportedly died from opium poisoning at the age of thirty-eight.

After several weeks of being exposed to psychiatry as a profession, it occurred to me that there is something intrinsically wrong with the profession. Psychiatry can not successfully provide treatment for persons with mental or emotional disorders unless the profession comes to grips with the true nature of the human. I had learned from my journey that humans are fundamentally spiritual beings having a physical experience while incarnated as human beings; we are here to learn and grow; when our physical life is over we will make the transition back to our natural spiritual state. Of this I am certain. Psychiatry cannot succeed as a profession unless it proceeds with the understanding that we are essentially spiritual beings.

After spending several weeks at Duke Medical Center as an outpatient, I was enrolled in the Duke University Preventive Approach to Cardiology (DUPAC) program. Although the DUPAC program was designed for patients surviving organic cardiovascular problems, heart attacks, open heart surgery, and such, the doctors decided to put me in the program because I had all the physical manifestations of someone who had had a massive heart attack. Yet no organic cause could be identified. I was a medical anomaly. The doctors also put me in the DUPAC program because they did not know what else to do with me. I was grateful that they did put me in the program, though. Through my participation in the program I would find—indirectly—the most important answers to my questions.

The DUPAC program was dedicated to creating permanent lifestyle changes for its participants, and I certainly needed a lifestyle change. The program consisted of exercising daily, eating a proper diet, and attending lectures on life renewal. I was being motivated physically, mentally, and emotionally to get back on course with my life. I even stopped drinking for the several weeks I was there.

One bright and sunny November morning, I was walking around DUPAC's outdoor track. I was feeling much better about myself since entering the program. Another DUPAC patient, an older man in his sixties, began to walk with me. We had just attended a lecture on Type A personalities—individuals inclined to have cardiac-related illnesses due to their high-strung psychological makeup and lifestyle. He told me his story as we walked.

"You know, like most everyone else in this program, I'm a Type A, or at least I was. My business used to mean everything to me. It drove my life although I used to think I drove it. I didn't think about anything else; family and friends came second. I was totally absorbed with business; it was my one and only gauge of being successful in life. You know the first thing I did when I got out of the hospital? I didn't tell anybody. I just took a sleeping bag and some camping provisions, and I drove alone up to a mountain where I used to camp as a kid.

I spent the night just looking up at the stars and realizing how wonderful the universe is."

I watched the radiant expression on this man's face, the gleam in his eyes, and realized we had a lot in common. He recognized the same thing in me. He continued, "Everyone around me thought that I was acting strange, but I didn't care. I saw things that I could never explain. You have to have been there to know what I am talking about." He looked at me intently. "You know what I'm talking about. I can tell. You've been there too."

"I want to hear the rest of your story," I said. "I did the same thing that you talked about. The first chance I had to be by myself, I went up to Pennsylvania where I grew up, and I went to the top of a mountain. I sat there at night, looking up at the stars. What made you decide to do it?"

"Well," he continued, "I had suffered a massive heart attack at my desk. I don't remember anything else until I watched the medics wheeling me out of the ambulance and into the emergency room. The only problem was I was watching them from a position above my body. I was out of my body looking down on the scene. The next thing I knew I was in this tunnel going toward a bright light, feeling totally peaceful and serene. I saw things that are beyond description, things that I still can't talk about."

I was so shocked at what he had just told me that I grabbed him by the arm and stopped him in his tracks.

"That happened to you?" I exclaimed. "The same thing happened to me, too. I thought I was the only one who had an experience like that. I thought I was going crazy, but you seem perfectly normal to me, and you're telling me that this happened to you. Have you told anyone else about this?"

"Oh, sure. Everyone thought that I was crazy, hallucinating or whatever from medication, so I just stopped talking. Then I mentioned it to a nurse here one day, and she understood what I was talking about. She recommended, off the record, that I go over to the college campus and speak to the people at the Rhine Institute. Have you talked to them yet?"

"Talk to who?" I responded, "I've talked to a lot of doctors here, but I never heard of the Rhine Institute."

"Well, go talk to this nurse. She'll set up an appointment for you. I met Dr. Rao over there. Go see him. I guarantee you will get a lot from meeting him."

I thanked him profusely, realizing that we had a connection few others had. I headed off the exercise track in search of the nurse.

"I was right about you," he called out to me. "I could tell you had been there too."

I spotted the nurse as soon as I entered the DUPAC Center. "I just met this other patient. We had similar experiences. He says you know something about this. He had a meeting with Dr. Rao, which he says you arranged. I want a meeting with him as soon as possible." I said all this, breathlessly. She smiled knowingly, stepped into her office, and dialed a number.

"You are in luck. Dr. Rao can see you at noon today. Can you fit that into your schedule?" she said, anticipating my response.

I had some free time before my noon appointment with Dr. Rao, so I stopped at the Duke chapel. I had sat in prayer and meditation in this chapel many times over the previous six weeks, wondering where my spiritual journey was leading me, wondering if the answers I sought would be found at Duke. I had walked through one of the greatest medical centers in the country and then across the commons of one of the greatest universities, and despite the accumulation of knowledge that existed in these university buildings, nothing had answered my most troubling questions about what I had experienced. Perhaps Dr. Rao at the Rhine Institute would have the answers.

I boarded a crowded bus for my appointment with Dr. Rao. The bus was full of students commuting to classes at the East Campus. While they chatted amicably, I was in my own world. Once off the bus I asked for directions and eventually stood across the street from 402 North Buchanan Boulevard. The two-story white framed building, which housed the Institute for Parapsychology, was across the street from the campus, literally on the fringe of the academic community geographically and metaphysically.

I felt somewhat uncomfortable and nervous as I knocked on the door. It opened slowly making creepy, creaking sounds; it needed to be oiled. A woman eyed me curiously as I announced my appointment with Dr. Rao. The building appeared to have been built as a professor's home before it was converted into offices. I was shown a seat in what must at one time have been the family sitting room, but which was now converted into a library. I scanned the bookshelves and noticed a collection of *The Journal of Parapsychology*. I opened one. *The Journal of Parapsychology* described itself as a scientific quarterly dealing with extrasensory perception, psychokinetic effects, and related topics. The editor was Doctor K. Ramakrishna Rao.

I started to get anxious. Had I entered the *Twilight Zone* again? The building was strangely silent, and I was pacing now, not comfortable that I was meeting Dr. Rao. Frankly, it was his middle name that bothered me: Ramakrishna! I was soon having a full-blown anxiety attack, mostly because of my cultural ignorance. I would later learn that *ramakrishna* means "religious teacher" in Hindi, but at the time I envisioned myself getting sucked into some brainwashing cult or the *Hare Krishnas,* spending the rest of my life chanting for donations in airports.

When Dr. Rao entered the room, I was even less confident. Dr. Rao was from India. I started to think this was a big mistake and was about to excuse myself. I had come to Duke to get facts, hard, cold scientific facts concerning what I experienced. I had somehow arrived at the Institute for Parapsychology under the incorrect impression that I was going to meet some scientific type who was going to give me a scientific explanation for my experience. I did not expect to be greeted by Dr. Rao. Suddenly, however, I had a change of heart.

I sensed that Dr. Rao was a man of peace, contentment, and enlightenment. The medical and scientific community had disappointed me. Perhaps Dr. Rao did know something those other doctors did not. I decided to stay for our meeting. For some reason, I trusted Dr. Rao. He apologized for not being prepared in advance to meet me since he was not sure exactly why I had requested this meeting. I explained that I had met another patient in the DUPAC program who had an unusual experience that he had shared with Dr. Rao. I believed I had a similar experience and thought maybe he could offer me insight. He gazed at me knowingly. "Yes, go on. Tell me about what you experienced."

"I passed out at my place of business and was picked up by an ambulance. While I was in the ambulance I felt like I kind of, you know, I kind of left my body and looked down on it while the EMTs were working on it. I felt like I was not in my body, but above it, looking down."

I wanted to cringe when I realized that I had told him something that sounded so insane. He shook his head seemingly as an acknowledgment that he believed me. I sensed that he had heard this account many times before. He simply said: "Yes, go on."

I wanted to stop right there with my story, not to go on, thinking he would never understand the next part.

"Well, go on." He encouraged me, "What happened next?"

"Well, I left the ambulance, you know, without my body. I felt that I myself left the ambulance, but I was now detached from my body, as if I had an identity that superseded my physical body. You know what I mean?"

"Yes." He said, nodding. "Please go on."

"Next I noticed my Rolex watch was missing, because it was on my body and I was no longer in my body." I looked at Dr. Rao quizzically, realizing how strange my conversation was getting. He encouraged me to continue.

Dr. Rao conveyed to me that he deserved my trust, so I opened up. I told him about meeting my friend who had been killed in Vietnam, about entering the tunnel. I told him about traveling through the tunnel and being absorbed by a radiant, indescribable light. I went on and on, telling my story, revealing myself to this stranger. I felt that Dr. Rao believed and understood everything I was telling him. I sensed he was not hearing this strange story for the first time. He knew I was reluctant to share this episode because he continually encouraged me.

I must have talked for over an hour. Once I got going, I relived the experience in detail. Finally, I ran out of things to say. I just stopped and looked at him blankly, looking for his response.

"The first thing I want you to know is that you are not going crazy," he said. I felt an incredible weight lift from my shoulders. "You had this experience, no doubt, and it is very real for you. Now you must come to terms with it and decide how you are going to get on with your life in view of this experience."

I felt a glow through my whole body. "You are not the only one who has had an experience like this. You are not alone. There are many others. Our files are full of reports of what you experienced."

There were others who shared my experience! Why didn't I know this before? Why was everyone keeping this experience such a big secret? Dr. Rao continued, "What happened to you is called a near-death experience."

He went on to describe the various stages of the experiences that have been reported by near-death survivors. He explained that work in this field was being conducted by a small group of scholars and scientists investigating the phenomena. I began to take notes as Dr. Rao mentioned the names of several doctors, universities, and research groups that could provide me with more information about the near-death experience. My meeting with Dr. Rao lasted for two hours, and at the time it was the most important meeting of my life. As I thanked him profusely and walked out I had that feeling, again, of being reborn.

Four and one-half months had passed since my near-death experience. During that time, I sometimes believed that I might be going crazy, mostly because I was trying to deny the reality of the experience, to make it not exist, especially when I was overwhelmed by it. I was hoping the psychiatrists at Duke could relieve me of this hallucination. It would have been so much easier to go back to my old life, drinking, drugging, womanizing, and partying like there was no tomorrow, no afterlife. However, as hard as I tried, the experience would not go away. All the debates I had with myself were futile. I could never overcome the power of the experience, the enormity of its content; nor could I deny its reality.

If I had awakened in the hospital with the entire experience before me, I probably would have imploded from sensory overload. I would have burned out mentally; I would have become a zombie. However, I remembered Dan's parting words: "You must remember this experience. This is not a dream."

During the months following the experience, I initially recalled all the major steps and events, but as time went on, the details of the experience became more vivid. For this reason alone, it became impossible to write off the experience as a hallucination. I was processing this experience in a way similar to the workings of a computer. When I traveled through the various stages of the experience, the master program of my own inner computer had to be readjusted so that I could function effectively in my spiritual state. Every thought, event, episode, or piece of information that became part of my experience since the beginning of my creation was restored and made available to me.

As part of this process, I was imbued with knowledge and insights that I had previously learned as a spiritual being but had forgotten during my earthly life. I could remember when each of these steps took place during the experience. For example, when I was embraced by the light, I was aware that I was absorbing universal knowledge. During this part of the experience I thought: "Oh, yes, of course. Why had I forgotten this?" I felt the energy flowing into my spirit; I felt information get stored that I would later be able to recall.

When I had been recovering in the hospital, I could pull up the "directory" of all the major events of my experience, but I could not get into each directory at that point. This was a practical aspect of the near-death experience, designed to allow me to deal with the major steps of the experience itself before I attempted to recall or pull up the directories to retrieve more specific information.

What is missing in this computer analogy is the fact that the experience consisted of an incredible energy that emanated from a loving and caring Creator. Above all, the experience was for me a manifestation of God's love for mankind. The experience was an episode of strong emotions of love, peace, contentment, serenity, and joy. Most of these emotions were new to me. I couldn't remember ever experiencing joy before. . . .

As I walked back across the Duke campus, I thought the problem for the Institute of Parapsychology in its search for the nature of man is that the energy of the spirit is not identifiable in materialistic or scientific terms. Consequently, most scientists do not accept parapsychology as a pure science. Even so, I felt a vibrant energy source traveling through my body, an energy source that I did not realize existed in me before the experience. The source of that energy is the Divine Creator. The energy itself is the active state of the spirit manifesting within me. I thought of myself as a soul, as a spiritual self, propelled by the energy of the spirit. I recognized that as a human I consisted of a body and a soul and that, at the moment of death, the soul separates from the body, propelled by the energy of the spirit. I was beginning to understand the nature of my being.

The most important issues that I came to Duke to resolve were not going to be answered in the medical center or in the university. After all the physical exams and medical tests were conducted, after all the bodily fluids were tapped and examined, after all the X-rays and monitors were evaluated, the conclusions were the same. There was no organic cause detected that could account for my near-death episode. Based on accepted scientific medical theories and practices, there was no explanation for what had happened. In medical terms, what I experienced was a syndrome, an episode, an event, but not otherwise definable in scientific terms. So I was left in the dark without answers from the medical and scientific community.

It's true I avoided discussing the near-death experience with the doctors; but then, no one asked me if I had experienced anything unusual when I had come so close to death. I remembered the nurse's admonishment, "If you don't stop talking that nonsense, we are going to have to call the psychiatrist in here." If I had not stopped talking, would I have been treated for hallucinations? Certainly, drugs would have been prescribed once it was determined that I was not already on drugs. If there had been procedures in place at the hospital for staff members to inquire about what a patient may have experienced, would I have been treated differently? If the hospital personnel were trained and familiar with the fact that people close to death do have these spiritual near-death experiences, would I have been able to come to terms with my situation sooner? If I had discussed my experience with one of the doctors or psychiatrists at Duke, would they have referred me to Dr. Rao? Not likely, since the Institute for Parapsychology was not officially accepted or recognized by the medical community.

My journey of four and one-half months in search of answers had taken me to three hospitals and dozens of doctors, psychiatrists, and psychologists. However, it was not the medical or scientific community that had the answers. The answers came from Dr. K. Ramakrishna Rao. The medicine I needed to continue my healing process was a mystical pill, found in the inspired words of Dr. Rao. He confirmed for me that I was not going crazy, that I was not alone, that many others had experienced the same kind of near-death episode.

I was beginning to recognize that what had happened to me on the evening of July 2 was a powerful and life-transforming event, a spiritual event. What appeared to be a curse was really a gift from heaven. I would now be able to get on with my life with full acceptance of this life-changing event. Besides, I had been told in the spiritual world that I was coming back to perform my newly-assigned mission in life, so it was time to begin performing it. Or so I thought.

CHAPTER 18

THE EPIPHANY

November 1984

Look what you people have done to us!
You have convinced us that we are alcoholics
and that our lives are unmanageable. Having
reduced us to a state of absolute helplessness,
you now declare that none but a higher power
can remove our obsession. Some of us won't
believe in God, others can't, and still others
that do believe that God exists have no faith
whatever that He will perform this miracle.
Yes, you've got us over the barrel, all right—
but where do we go from here?
(from "The Twelve Steps," Alcoholics Anonymous)

I returned to the DUPAC office to thank the nurse
who had arranged my visit. I commented on how much
better I was feeling since I had been in the DUPAC

program. I mentioned that I had stopped drinking. Since none of the physicians had ever indicated on my records that alcoholism was possibly one of my problems, the nurse had no reason to suspect that I was an alcoholic. Her response to my comment about not drinking was to tell me that it was not necessary to abstain from alcohol in the DUPAC program.

"As a matter of fact," she continued, "research had shown that people who had two alcoholic drinks per day during their adult lives were less likely to have cardiac conditions than people who never drank alcohol." The research may have been correct, but where did they find these people who would only have two drinks per day? I had been looking for an excuse to continue to drink and to somehow incorporate my drinking into the new and more spiritual being that I intended to be. I had been praying to God that he would allow me to learn how to drink "like a gentleman" as part of my new and more spiritual lifestyle.

That evening, I ate in a French restaurant and planned on limiting my intake to two drinks. It is amazing how an alcoholic can re-define terms. In this case, I wanted to order a bottle of red wine with dinner, but I certainly couldn't drink only two glasses and leave the rest. By the time I had finished dinner, I had consumed two bottles of wine, somehow rationalizing two bottles to equal two drinks.

During dinner, I pondered how I was going to perform my mission in life. First, I would return to New York. I had been keeping a list of friends and business associates who I believed needed my help. Based on the visions I had received concerning their futures, I decided on a plan to alter the course of their futures by meeting with them and insisting that they follow my advice.

Dr. Rao validated my experience, allowing me to get on with my life. However, I was attempting to reduce his validation to such simplistic terms that I began to think that I was invincible. I began to believe that God had chosen me for some unexplainable reason to set about changing my future, my friends' futures, and the future of the world. Certainly, I believed that my intentions were honorable, but I failed to understand God's plan for me. Buoyed by the wine, I had my own egotistical vision of altering the future and expecting God's acceptance of what I did.

For the next several days, I continued to drink excessively. During this time, I called my business associates, lawyers, accountants, and friends in New York and arranged meetings with each of them. When I arrived in New York several days later, my business meetings turned out to be disastrous due to my excessive drinking. When I finally met with friends, they expressed concern that I had gone off the deep end. Frustrated and defeated in my initial attempt to return to a normal life and regroup, I decided to return to Duke. I was convinced that I would find a way to continue to drink "like a gentleman" because I could not imagine a normal life without alcohol.

My return flight to Duke required a change of planes in Washington, D.C. At the last minute I decided not to get on the plane to Raleigh-Durham. Instead, I took a cab from the airport to my favorite Washington bar, Ebbitt's Grille. After having a few drinks, I spent much of the afternoon walking around the streets of Washington trying to understand what was happening in my life. I knew that I couldn't go on with my life in my present state of mind. I found it very difficult to think of my near-death experience as a gift when I was having so much trouble integrating it into my life. I could not keep going with one foot on Earth and the other in the spiritual world. I became angry with God for leaving me in such a hapless state, because He did not allow me to learn how to drink "like a gentleman" so that I could get on with my normal life. Then I was angry with God because I couldn't leave my physical existence. I wanted to reexperience being a spirit again, to float free, relieved of the physical body and its pain. However, I was trapped in my physical body. God had given me one option: to remain on Earth and complete my mission. Any other choice was not mine to make. Suicide was not an option. I learned from my experience that suicide should not be an option for anyone. My only option was to get on with my life.

Since my meeting with Dr. Rao, I could no longer debate the reality of what I had experienced on July 2. It would have been easier to accept the episode as a hallucination or a dream, but that was now impossible. Since the experience was real, I had to face the fact that I had been given a spiritual gift and a mission in life. To perform that mission, I would first have to recover from my alcoholism. My drinking days were over. They had to be. I was resigned to the fact that I had to stop drinking, but how was I going to do it?

It was difficult enough dealing with my own problems, but being in Washington caused me to focus on the state of the country and the world. Much of what happened in the world—politically, financially, economically, and even spiritually—emanated from decisions that were made by the political and power brokers in Washington. Unfortunately, from the perspective of my near-death experience, everything about the way the power brokers ran the government and the world was all wrong. Why did God choose me to have a near-death experience? If He wanted mankind to recognize His plan, why hadn't He recalled all the politicians and powerbrokers and reintroduced them to their true missions in life according to His plan? Perhaps then we would all be able to begin to live in a brave new world.

After walking around Washington for hours, I found myself back at Ebbitt's Grille staring across the bar at a stranger. The stranger was my own reflection in the mirror. It was evening, and the bar was filled with customers standing shoulder to shoulder ordering drinks and conversing loudly around me. Although I had been drinking beer all afternoon, now I ordered an Irish Mist. I raised the glass to the stranger across the bar, somehow knowing that this was going to be my last drink. I swallowed the last of the liquor in the glass and put it back down on the bar. As I continued to stare across the bar, I felt a surge of energy move up through my body. I was beginning to have a spiritual experience. I stood up, breathed in deeply, and exhaled relief. This was a sacred moment I would remember for all my life.

Suddenly, the noise of the place dimmed and I no longer heard any sounds. It was as if time had slowed down. Everyone around me seemed to be suspended in a motionless state. I turned full circle viewing all the strangers in the bar, and then I turned back to the bar again and stared at the stranger. I realized it had been twenty years to the month since I had first begun to drink. I was the stranger in the mirror, a stranger to myself. Whoever I really was, as a spiritual and human being, had been lost to me for those twenty years. Suddenly, a roaring mechanical sound moved by me. The scene around me melted into a funnel of shimmering walls, and I was staring into a tunnel. The dim image at the end of the tunnel was my mirror image staring back at me. I was in the tunnel again, the same as I had been five months ago. Perhaps I was being called back. I always thought of that night in July as an orientation program; maybe my real death was now imminent.

I didn't want to leave the physical world from a bar, so I moved quickly through the crowd to the door. I must have been a menacing sight; I watched as people moved away from me quickly. I pushed myself through the door and out into the night. I wanted to be under the stars. I wanted to return to the Other Side.

I began to walk across 15th Street and along the side of the Treasury Building. As much as I had been drinking, I should have been stumbling and falling, but I was not; nor had I passed out after several drinks, as I had been doing since my near-death experience. God had allowed me to go on my last drinking binge for the past several days so I would get His message. So that I could get on with my life, I had been asking God to allow me to drink "like a gentleman," and now He was giving me His answer: Forget it!

I felt like I was being lifted down the street by an invisible force. I walked down 15th Street, across E Street, and onto the lawn of the Ellipse. As I crossed the park moving away from the Treasury Building and the White House, I passed the homeless people, alcoholics, and drug abusers making their homes on park benches and in cardboard shelters. What kind of a country had we become that we turned our heads away from our brothers and sisters who had fallen on such hard times?

And here I was among them, moving across the Ellipse, one foot in front of the other, guided where I did not know. Like the vagrants, I was not in control. I was being spiritually guided, but these were not the spirits of the bottle—not this time. I had left them back in Ebbitt's Grille.

For twenty years, I had not been in control. I used to think I was, but every time I made a decision or a plan, I had a glass or bottle in my hand. When I started drinking as an eighteen-year-old, it never dawned on me that the spirits in the bottle would edge out my own spirit. I did not realize how subtly and powerfully alcohol would take over my life.

As I walked across Constitution Avenue and into a darkened tree-lined path, I thought how I had lost control of my thoughts and actions, of my destiny. Now it was time to gain it back, and oddly, I would gain it by letting go. I had to turn over my control to God who was now guiding me. As I walked through the dark path, I was not alone. He was guiding me. I realized that my life was not about to end, but that I had another chance, a new beginning. My drinking days were over; the twenty-year saga had come to an end. I had to recover physically, spiritually, mentally, and emotionally. I knew what I had to do. Now that I was beginning to discover my true self, I was determined to move forward in my life with a strong spirit. Reunited with my spirit, I would never again let it go.

I walked further along the darkened path until it opened into a clearing. I looked up into a sky of brilliant stars. I was overwhelmed with emotion. My journey had brought me to a rise of land that overlooked the Vietnam War Memorial. Again.

I stood again in front of the slab of granite bearing my friend's name. I thought back to the night of July 2, when I left my body in the ambulance and floated free to be greeted by Dan. That evening had been the start of a long and difficult path of spiritual discovery that was still only just beginning. It was no coincidence that I had been drawn back to this wall on this particular night. As I reached out to touch my friend's name on the wall, a shock of energy went through my body. I felt my body falling to the ground. I was now free of that body and floating above it.

I was enveloped in an intense light. I was in the presence of a great spiritual being. A booming voice filled the air; it was the most powerful voice I had ever heard. It was the voice of the Archangel Michael. I recognized that he was conveying a message of importance:

> Your forefathers created one nation under God, with liberty and justice for all. These were men of high ideals, spiritually guided and inspired to create a nation and a civilization to be admired and respected, to set an example for the rest of the world. In exercising their free will under God's guidance and direction, they created a Constitution and a Bill of Rights for every man, woman, and child to live in freedom in the pursuit of happiness. Yet these high-minded and spiritual men were soon replaced by others who, in the exercise of their free will, chose to put their egos before God and to joust with God's plan.
>
> You became a nation of spoilers, man against man, brother against brother, government against citizens, and the chosen nation became a warrior with and against other nations. You have become a nation of criminals and murderers. You murder in wars. You murder the innocent. You murder your children. Your leaders create laws to justify the murders, to attempt to make wrongs right, to rewrite morals and ethics to support your own earthbound greeds and desires.
>
> You have become a nation further and further from the spirit and the influence of God. You have created sciences and philosophies to support activities that only recognize earthbound realities, that not only refuse to recognize the spiritual nature of

man himself, but refuse to recognize even the existence of God.

You have taken God and His works of prayer and meditation out of your government, out of your institutions, out of your schools. You have done everything you can to deny His existence, and you find yourselves in a world filled with wars, hatred, starvation, and death, and you do not understand why the rest of the world does not follow your shining example.

You are a nation at war with itself, filled with hatred, prejudice, crime, drugs, and murder. Yet, when the few of you who do look to God ask Him why all these things are allowed to happen, you do not hear His answer.

You are members of the human race, universally created by God and given free will individually by divine right, and you would not wish to have it any other way. Yet every little act of free will that man has exercised from the beginning of time, that was not in accordance with God's plan, multiplied in its impact and its negativity on the future of man. Every simple act of aggression multiplied into acts of world war. Every simple act of greed multiplied into worldwide human suffering and starvation. Every act of destruction of God's environment on Earth multiplied into destructive forces of nature—earthquakes, floods, pestilence; nuclear destruction and nuclear waste. Every act of violence escalated into acts of murder and the extermination of ethnic people for their appearance or beliefs.

Yet, God created a nation of high ideals for you to survive other empires and civilizations that crumbled into oblivion, for their leaders placed themselves as men above God, and now those empires and civilizations are but piles of dust or buried under the waters. You sit on the edge of the new millennium, poised for the future of mankind, and you are headed, like all great civilizations of the past, to be reduced to piles of dust, to be covered over by the waters.

Yet, God comes to you again, to appeal to you as a people, to appeal to you as a nation, to appeal to your leaders. His army of angels is visiting upon you with a life force of energy, a spiritual energy radiated by the Creator to all mankind. Many of you feel the vibrancy of His energy and His divine presence. He is communicating with you spiritually, telling you to raise yourselves to the level of spiritual transformation that is necessary for those of you who hear Him to spread His message and His energy, to recognize that He is coming.

Guided by prayer and meditation, all men, women, and children may answer His call, but it must be soon. Time is running out! The angels are coming! Do you hear them? Are you listening?

Are you listening?

As the Archangel Michael's message ended in a haunting echo, I began to float gently back down into my body. Several people were standing over it as it lay sprawled on the sidewalk at the base of the wall. Further away, I could see a team of EMTs with a gurney rushing toward my body. As my spiritual self reentered my body, I began to gasp for air. I felt an energy force of spirit move up, through, and out of my body. Then I realized that the gnawing feeling in my gut had also left my body; the feeling that had consumed me for so many years had disappeared. My compulsion to drink was gone! I found myself reunited with my body in a state of peace and serenity.

As the EMTs began to work on me, I felt a gentle breeze and heard the rustling of autumn leaves on the knoll. My last thoughts were of the message of the Archangel Michael, as his final words echoed through my ebbing state of consciousness, "Are you listening?"

Falling asleep, I responded, "I am! I am! I am!"

CHAPTER 19

THE RECOVERY

1984-1985

> Do you remember how electrical currents
> and "unseen waves" were laughed at? The
> knowledge about man is still in its infancy!
> —*Albert Einstein*

I was picked up by the EMTs and rushed to the hospital again. Again I was admitted into the hospital in a comatose state. Although I was wearing my Rolex watch and carrying a wallet full of IDs and credit cards, I was treated like a vagrant or one of the homeless due to my appearance. Apparently, PCP was the designer drug of choice among Washington's homeless. Assuming therefore that I also must have been on PCP, I was soon transferred to another hospital for admission and for psychiatric evaluation. Fortunately, upon recovering from my spiritual experience, I had the presence of mind to refuse to cooperate with the hospital attendants who were hell-bent on administering psychoactive drugs. During the three days that I was required to remain for observation, I refused medication. I was befriended by a younger patient who was quite enamored with my Rolex watch. In a moment of weakness, I consented to letting him try on the Rolex, and then in a flash he was gone from the hospital with my Rolex on his wrist.

It was only when I walked out of that hospital that my real recovery began. I spent the next four months in virtual seclusion in my apartment in New York City. I had spent twenty years drinking heavily and poisoning my system with drugs, both prescription and, occasionally, illegal. However, it was alcohol that was my preferred addiction. I learned during my experience that I had been born into this world with a thirst for love and knowledge that could only be satisfied by following a positive path. However, I traveled onto a negative path that turned my thirst for life into a craving for self-gratification. I learned that people like myself who become addicted to alcohol, drugs, or sex are subconsciously attempting to reconnect with our spiritual nature, but we venture onto a negative path that only leads to self-destruction. I had no choice but to return to a positive path in order to recover from my addictions. My daily activities consisted of waking up with dreams or visions from my near-death experience, followed by meditation. I breakfasted on whole-grain cereals and non-caffeinated herbal teas. I jogged to a health club owned by a friend, whose counsel I sought because I knew he had quit drinking several years previously. At the health club, I worked out on the exercise machines, then finished with several trips back and between the sauna and a cold shower. I sweated, and sweated, and sweated. I drank plenty of water to avoid dehydration and to purify my system of toxins.

I continued to take pills, but they were not prescribed by a doctor, nor were they illegal. They were vitamins. I took multivitamins and large amounts of B vitamins, including niacin for eliminating toxins. Constant exercise, sweating, and purging of my system helped rid my body of the alcoholic residues of twenty years. The vitamins and a healthy diet provided the nourishment I needed for a full recovery.

Despite the weather conditions of winter in New York, I spent these months constantly walking outdoors. I appreciated all kinds of weather, the cold, the wind, the rain, and the snow. An abandoned railroad line was very close to my apartment. Even though I was in New York City, I could walk along the abandoned and overgrown railroad line and find myself in a natural setting, reminiscent of the hikes I used to take in Pennsylvania.

Walking was therapeutic. First, the exercise helped me to recover physically and emotionally. Second, I did a lot of thinking while walking. I was not only processing the near-death experience; I was learning how to reconnect with my human existence on earth. During the initial recovery period, I had one foot on terra firma and one foot on the Other Side. I had to adjust to the fact that my return to actual death was not imminent, that I had to relearn to live on the planet, at least for a while. My near-death experience had been an orientation to the afterlife, but my final return to the afterlife was in a distant future. And I had to confront visions of future world events as well as events in my life.

I had the greatest difficulty in accepting the limitations of time and space. During my near-death experience, I had been shown future events in my personal life that I tried to "make happen" while I was still recovering. However, these events were not intended to take place on *my* schedule or at *my* urging or wishing. They were going to happen in God's time, not mine. Therefore, I had to adjust to living with patience—a rare commodity, particularly to someone living in New York City. I replaced the Rolex with a Timex diver's watch that I bought for $29.95. It kept perfect time. It had a stopwatch, an alarm, and a light, so I could see what time it was, even in the dark. I couldn't imagine how much it would have cost to get a Rolex that had all those options.

In March 1985 I returned to my home in the Hamptons and my nightclub business, which had reopened for the summer season with a St. Patrick's Day parade and fund-raiser party. The reopening of Marakesh for the summer season was a community event. Everyone showed up for this annual party as a kind of rite of spring.

During the reopening party, I positioned myself at the front entrance of the club and greeted patrons as they entered. It was important that I reintroduce myself to the community. Rumors had circulated about my brush with death and my hospitalizations, about my medical prognosis as well as my state of sanity. It was important to me that I let people know that I was back in the "real" world and healthy. The fund-raiser party was held approximately ninety days after I had put down my last drink in Ebbitt's Grille. I would not drink the night of the fund-raiser party, nor would I drink ever again, with God's help.

By April 1985 I felt that I was well along the road to recovery. Four months had passed since my second near-death experience—my epiphany at the Vietnam War Memorial. During the intervening time, I contemplated the meaning of my spiritual experiences, particularly the message from the Archangel Michael. I knew that at some future time I was supposed to rigorously pursue my "mission in life" as it was presented to me during my first near-death experience. I knew that it was of great importance for me to communicate Archangel Michael's message so that others could share its prophetic message. However, I had developed an understanding that all of these things would take time, according to a schedule not of my own making. Besides, I had to recover from the trauma that these spiritual experiences had created in my life.

I spent most of my days and nights working on my recovery. Having shunned the medical community, I was inspired in my recovery process. Living at my home in the Hamptons, I spent most of my time alone, but I was eagerly looking forward to attending the conference of the International Association for Near-Death Studies scheduled for April 12 and 13, 1985, at the University of Connecticut.

I had first heard about this group, known as IANDS, through Dr. Rao. IANDS was the only worldwide organization devoted to the study of the near-death experience. IANDS had been originally organized by a group of doctors and researchers primarily at the University of Virginia, where the pioneering work in near-death research was conducted as early as 1958 under the leadership of psychiatrist Ian Stevenson, M.D. Some of the earliest pioneers in near-death research were psychiatrists: Dr. Elisabeth Kübler-Ross, who wrote *On Death and Dying* in 1969; Dr. Raymond Moody, *Life After Life* in 1975; and Dr. George Ritchie, who wrote a recollection of his own near-death experience, *Return from Tomorrow,* in 1978.

In November 1977 Dr. Moody organized a meeting at the University of Virginia for twenty researchers who were studying near-death phenomena. The meeting resulted in the formation of the Association for the Scientific Study of Near-Death Phenomena, which was intended to serve as a data bank of near-death experiences. This organization provided the foundation for the International Association for Near-Death Studies (IANDS), which was founded in 1981 by some of the researchers, including Dr. Bruce Greyson, a psychiatrist; Dr. Kenneth Ring, a psychologist; and Dr. Michael Sabom, a cardiologist.

When IANDS was incorporated as a non-profit organization in 1981, its offices were moved to the University of Connecticut at Storrs. By then, the organization was expanded to include not only scholarly researchers, but also support groups for near-death experiencers and for other individuals interested in studying these experiences. IANDS had three goals: first, to encourage thoughtful exploration of all facets of the near-death experience; second, to provide reliable information about these subjects to experiencers, researchers, and the public; third, to serve as a contact point and community for people with particular interest in near-death and related experiences.

As I drove through Connecticut, I decided to observe the conference from a distance and not participate. I did not know at the time that my behavior was characteristic of someone who had survived a near-death experience. All I knew was that because of my treatment I had become disillusioned with the medical and scientific community. From the time I arrived in the emergency room on the evening of July 2, 1984, until I met with Dr. Rao four months later, no one in the medical community had considered the possibility that I may have had a near-death experience. In fact, doctors and nurses were ill-equipped in their training to be on the lookout for near-death experiences (NDEs) because the medical and nursing schools had no mention of NDEs in their curricula. Scientifically speaking, the existence or reality of NDEs could not be proven; therefore, they couldn't be included in the medical curriculum.

On the first evening of the conference I sat in the bleachers of the gymnasium, amazed that over 1,600 people had come to hear a medical doctor speak about death and dying. Dr. Elisabeth Kübler-Ross was born in Switzerland in 1926, and she graduated from medical school at the University of Zurich in 1957. She moved to the United States in 1958 and taught psychiatry while specializing in treating the terminally ill. In her book *Death and Dying* she described five psychological stages experienced by the dying: denial, anger, bargaining for time, grieving, and acceptance. She spoke with a heavy accent—and with great compassion.

Although this conference was about death and dying, Dr. Kübler-Ross's positive treatment of the subject was about life and living. She spoke for over two hours, and I was riveted to my seat listening to her describe how she had documented over 20,000 near-death experiences in twenty years of research. She remarked how the reports of near-death experiences had been viewed by skeptics as the product of diseased imaginings or deliberate fraud. The reports of experiencers came from all over the world, she noted. The near-death phenomena had become so common and irrefutable that she believed knowledge of NDEs would become common to the public in about fifty years—despite the fact that the researchers themselves encountered abuse and negativity from their colleagues.

Dr. Kübler-Ross explained that dying children experienced pre-death visions with characteristics similar to those experienced by near-death survivors. She had seen how the dying children often became the teachers to their parents, helping them cope with grief by understanding that death is the bridge that goes from this life to the next one. It seems that before these children died, they were given messages to help the surviving parents deal with the transition of their children to the afterlife.

Dr. Kübler-Ross hit home with me when she said that you truly had a near-death experience if you were no longer afraid of dying. This was true for me; I no longer feared death. I was not crazy about the prospect of suffering and pain leading up to the transition, which was a process I wished to avoid at all costs. However, at point of death, after the physical pain and suffering were over, the transition to the Other Side was painless. I knew this to be true from personal experience. It was not the fear of death that had brought me to the IANDS conference; it was the fear of not knowing how I was going to live on the Earth in the meantime.

On the second day of the conference, I attended workshops conducted by Dr. Bruce Greyson and Dr. Kenneth Ring. Although I listened intently, I avoided dialogue with the presenters. I stuck to my plan not to engage anyone in conversation. I was there to observe and not to participate. I learned that I was a *core* near-death experiencer in that I had experienced a majority of the characteristics usually reported by near-death survivors.

The IANDS literature listed the following stages of the near-death experience:

- A feeling that the self has left the body and is hovering overhead.
- Moving through a dark space or a tunnel.
- Experiencing intensely powerful emotions, ranging from bliss to terror.

- Encountering a light. It is usually described as golden or white, and as being magnetic and loving; occasionally it is perceived as a reflection of the fires of hell.
- Receiving some variant of the message: "It is not yet your time."
- Meeting others: maybe deceased loved ones, recognized from life or not; sacred beings; unidentified entities and/or beings of light; or sometimes symbols from one's own or other religious traditions.
- Having a life review, seeing and reexperiencing major and trivial events of one's life, sometimes from the perspective of the other people involved, and coming to some conclusion about the adequacy of that life and what changes are needed.
- Having a sense of understanding everything, of knowing how the universe works.
- Reaching a boundary: a cliff, fence, water, or some kind of barrier that may not be crossed if one is to return to life.
- In some cases, entering a city or library.
- Rarely, receiving previously unknown information about one's life, i.e., adoption or hidden parentage, deceased siblings.
- The decision to return may be voluntary or involuntary. If voluntary, it's usually associated with unfinished responsibilities.
- Returning to the body.

IANDS literature listed thirteen characteristics of the near-death experience. Although researchers used various formulas to weigh the characteristics of near-death experiences, there was no doubt that I had what was considered a core experience. Twelve of the thirteen characteristics were definitely a part of my experience. I could relate to every one of the characteristics with the exception of reaching a boundary. I did not reach a boundary or barrier that could not be crossed if I were to return to life. Rather, it was clearly conveyed to me that I was going back to my earthly life. I was not given an option to hang around for a while to make up my own mind. I was clearly kicked out. I probably wasn't invited to stay, considering my level of spirituality—or lack of it. It was as if they had stamped me on the forehead "REJECT" and sent me back. I have never been kicked out of a better place, but I had been sent back to complete my mission in life, whatever that was.

Based on my NDE, I would have added two more characteristics to the IANDS list:

- Prophetic visions, sometimes of a personal nature, sometimes involving global events.
- Music and sounds, sometimes ethereal music and sounds, including chimes or crystal-like sounds.

I had the most difficulty processing the first additional characteristic: being shown future events in my life as well as in the world. However, since these predicted global and personal events had not taken place by the time of the conference, I pondered the possibility that those visions on their own might have been hallucinations. I could no longer deny that the experience happened, that it was a real and true event in my life. But I was trying to rationalize and dismiss the more unpleasant visions, to dismiss them as dreams or hallucinations. Conversely, during the first several months following the experience, I found myself trying to make these positive visions of my future happen. I soon learned that I could fail miserably at trying to control the future and making things happen according to a time schedule that I had set for myself. By the time of the conference, I recognized that if these future visions were going to take place, it was going to be in God's time and not in mine.

The second characteristic that was not listed by the IANDS material, but that was definitely a part of my experience, was the presence of heavenly music, particularly of chimes and crystals. I attended a sound laboratory session conducted by Dr. Joel Funk, a psychologist from Plymouth State College in New Hampshire. During this workshop, I completed a questionnaire designed for near-death experiencers who had heard sounds or music. Then I sat before a tape deck with earphones on. The instructions indicated that I would hear fifteen musical selections, each approximately one minute in length. I was to score each selection as it related to the mood or sounds I experienced during my NDE. I listened to the first several selections; some of these would be considered classical arrangements while the others sounded ethereal. I was disappointed initially; none of the selections had any relevance to my experience.

The fifth selection triggered an instant recall of my experience. I sat back with my eyes closed, meditating on the experience, emotionally feeling as if I was re-experiencing the other side of reality. The music brought tears to my eyes. I now knew why I had spent the last several months on a maniacal buying spree of ethereal-sounding music. I was subconsciously trying to reconnect with my experience by reexperiencing the sounds, and now I was hearing them.

Several other selections triggered memories of specific parts of my experience because they so closely simulated the actual sounds I had heard. In total, I rated five of the fifteen selections as similar to or sounding almost exactly like what I had heard during my experience. Although no earthly music could compare in intensity to the heavenly music that I had experienced, these five selections triggered such a strong recall that I felt myself swelling with emotion and spiritual awareness.

The sound laboratory experiment was an important validation for me that added tremendously to my healing process. It was validating to learn that many of the characteristics I had experienced were similar to those experienced by others. I was aware that certain medical and scientific skeptics were trying to provide biological explanations for NDEs. They theorized that the various stages reported by NDEers were actually visualizations created by the mind in life-threatening situations. The introduction of sounds and music into the NDE equation presents an even more baffling problem for the skeptics, unless they are going to propose that the brains of NDEers are somehow pre-programmed with the same musical arrangements, which are somehow triggered during the NDE experience. Who then composed the music?

It was easy for me to understand how NDE skeptics would attempt to rationalize a biological basis for the experience, that they would argue that NDE survivors shared similar experiences because of some mental pre-programming triggered at clinical or near-death situations. Prior to my near-death experience, I was inclined to be skeptical. I also lived in a world of alcohol and drugs and fast-lane living, where friends boasted about their hallucinatory experiences. I would have been the first street-smart expert to dismiss an account of a near-death experience as a hallucination. Not anymore. In the ranks of near-death survivors, there are no disbelievers.

One intriguing proposition is that near-death survivors from all over the world (never previously knowing each other or about NDEs) all shared similar experiences. Furthermore, as I learned at the conclusion of the sound laboratory workshop, I and other near-death experiencers consistently gave high scores to the same sound selections. Most of the other selections, many of which were other classical, liturgical, or ethereal selections, were consistently scored low or zero. The workshop confirmed for me that I did hear sounds and music during my NDE and that these were similar to those heard by others. I was now confident that the NDE is a multi-dimensional experience of sights, sounds, and moods experienced by thousands of people from different backgrounds, beliefs, and religions.

At the end of the conference, I drove back to the Hamptons having experienced another level of healing, and confident that what I had experienced on July 2, 1984, was a real and true event. Meanwhile, I had to get on with my life. I had businesses to run, bills to pay, and tax returns to file. I was still haunted by the visions of the future. Were they real or hallucinations? Whatever they were, I decided to let things take their course. My health was returning, so it did not appear that I was going back to the Other Side anytime soon. I decided that I would mentally file the NDE away. Strong-willed, I believed I could put the experience behind me and get on with my life. . . .

CHAPTER 20

A SOBERING TRANSITION

The human mind is capable of excitement
without the application of gross and violent
stimulants; and he must have a very faint
perception of its beauty and dignity who
does not know this.

—*William Wordsworth*

When I returned home from the IANDS conference
in April 1985, I thought of my near-death experience as
a singular event. Although I knew I still had a lot of processing to do, I thought that everything would eventually get back to normal, whatever that was. What I was
not prepared for was the fact that the near-death experience was not a single event, but the beginning of a
continuously evolving spiritual journey that would
guide and influence me for the rest of my life.

The most immediate physiological impact of my
near-death experience was that it cured me of my alcoholism. In November 1984 I had my last drink in

Ebbitt's Grille in Washington, D.C., before my walk to the Vietnam War Memorial where I was miraculously healed of my twenty-year-long craving for alcohol. I claim I was healed of my alcoholism as a result of my spiritual experience, but it is a conditional claim because nobody is ever really "cured" of alcoholism. I was only cured of my *active* addiction. Alcoholism and other addictions are lifelong diseases that require constant maintenance and spiritual support. Yet, I avoided seeking professional help or attending Alcoholics Anonymous meetings because I had become disillusioned with any kind of professional or medical help.

I awoke one morning in May 1985 and realized that it had been six months since I had stopped drinking. I had been counting the days. I wanted to celebrate this occasion, but I planned on spending the day alone working in my new vegetable garden. I had taken up gardening because I found it to be very therapeutic, watching the small plants grow from seedlings. I had also become a vegetarian since my NDE. Later in the morning, I met a friend at the 7-11 coffee counter; I knew that he had been going to AA meetings. I proudly announced to him that I was celebrating six months of sobriety that very day. He responded by inviting me to go to an AA meeting that night, and I decided to go.

In the evening, I went to a local church and walked down the steps into the basement. I sat by the exit door and listened to people talk about their drinking problems while each one of them chain-smoked cigarettes. Soon a cloud of smoke filled the room. I couldn't breathe and left the meeting thinking that those in attendance were sicker than I. I recalled a statistic that for every person who died from drugs, three died from alcohol, and three hundred died from smoking-related illnesses. Unbeknownst to me at the time, AA also had non-smoker meetings. Several more years went by and I managed to exist without AA, but I had the support of my NDE to guide me in maintaining sobriety.

I still owned the nightclub, but I was no longer actively involved in the fast-lane nightlife or even desirous of remaining in the business. My personal mission was to improve my personal and business reputation in the community. Prior to my NDE, it was rumored that I was involved in a cocaine drug cartel. These rumors didn't bother me at the time, because I was not actually involved in drug dealing. Besides, at the time the idea that I was a drug lord actually added to the glamorization of my reputation among people who were drawn to the disco nightlife.

By the summer of 1986, my more positive reputation had improved to the degree that a county official appointed me as chairman of a "Say No To Drugs" weekend events program in the Hamptons. Just prior to the event, a county policeman was shot-gunned in the face at point-blank range by a motorist who had been disgruntled over receiving a ticket from the policeman. I wanted to do something for the policeman while he was recovering in the hospital from the near-fatal shooting, so I arranged to have the proceeds from the weekend event donated to the policeman's family.

Shortly after the county policeman was shot, a state trooper apprehended his assailant. Later, this same trooper was assisting a motorist at the side of the road and was accidentally run over and killed by a passing car. His widow and a young son, age 6, survived the trooper. I could not grant the deceased trooper's boy his ultimate wish to bring back his dad, but I did grant the boy another wish. I held a fundraiser at Club Marakesh, and we provided an all-expense paid trip for the boy and his mother to Disney World. While creating these fund-raising events for worthy causes, I was mindful of the future vision concerning the creation of the Mission of Angels Foundation. I perceived that these events would provide the groundwork for the kind of good works that would become one of the goals of the Mission of Angels.

During this period, many people came to me with their drinking problems because they saw that I had quit drinking. I couldn't exactly advise them to go out and have a near-death experience to cure their drinking problems. Since I was not participating in a support group myself, I was not prepared to offer them any advice, so I referred them to the Seafield Center, the local alcoholism treatment center, located two blocks from Club Marakesh. I began to think that God was keeping me in the nightclub business so that I could refer problem drinkers to Seafield Center. If I had to deal with an unruly customer who appeared to have a drinking problem, and I sensed that I had an opportunity to intervene, I would send that person down the street to the Seafield Center.

After a few years I realized that my nightclub business was declining, and Seafield's business was booming. It was a sign of the times. The Baby Boomers were finding recovery after years of drinking and medicating themselves. The nightclubs and bars in the Hamptons were obviously doing less business while the country churches in the Hamptons had their parking lots filled during AA meetings. Mercedes-Benzes and Porsches mingled with pickup trucks and cars just shy of the junkyard.

Several years after I quit drinking, I visited a friend who was a patient at Seafield Center. My visit happened to coincide with an AA meeting that I decided to attend with my friend. During the meeting, I realized that I had much to learn from AA. I realized that AA's spiritual program of recovery was similar to my own plan, which was spiritually inspired. I egotistically assumed that AA was on the right track if it were doing the same thing I was; only I was trying to recover in isolation. I do not recommend recovering alone to anyone.

My becoming involved in AA came at a transition point in my life. I had recently returned from a vacation with a girlfriend, and our relationship had run its course. Near-death survivors have a difficult time maintaining pre-NDE personal relationships. Alcoholics have a difficult time maintaining pre- and post-recovery relationships. Statistically, the survival rate of post-NDE relationships is less than twenty percent, and the survival rate of relationships for people in recovery from addictions is not much better. People who get through these transitions make significant changes in their lives, and the significant other person is not always accepting of these changes. Consequently, the relationships falter and perish in many, if not most, cases.

Concerned that I had reached an impasse in my recovery, I decided to give AA another try, so I attended another meeting and stood by the exit door. There is a belief in the spiritually-based AA program that there are no coincidences. When the meeting was over, I stayed behind to talk with Paul, a retired undercover narcotics cop. He would eventually become my AA sponsor. Larry, a retired federal agent who used to frequent my night-club, joined us. Then Ken, whose face had been terribly disfigured, also sat with us. Ken was blind and obviously in a lot of physical pain, but he was there to help me deal with my problems. It was the first opportunity I had to meet Ken, who was the county policeman who had painfully survived being shotgunned in the face at point-blank range.

Shortly after I began attending AA meetings, I spent a week at the Caron Foundation's "Chit Chat" Retreat in Wernersville, Pennsylvania. I went there to attend an intensive recovery program that was designed for Adult Children of Alcoholics. I still had a lot of processing to do to recover from the loss of my dad and the disintegration of my family as a result of his alcoholism. The Chit Chat program was like emotional open heart surgery, designed to allow each participant to let go of all the grief and pain that was stuffed inside as a result of being the child of an alcoholic. I realized that part of my mission in life was to break the genetic chain of alcoholism that linked me to my father, my grandfather, and his father all the way back to ancient times in Ireland.

My introduction to AA and my personal commitment to embrace the AA program was an important part of my recovery from alcoholism. It was also a prerequisite for me to be ready for the next stages in my mission in life. I had to be sober and mentally, emotionally, and spiritually prepared for the road ahead of me, for the future visions would soon begin to unfold into reality.

During the autumn of 1986, I was inexplicably drawn to the barrier beach in the Hamptons to watch as an apparently insignificant scouring of the beach began to grow larger and larger, removing an ever-increasing volume of sand. Although little public notice seemed to have been given to this erosion, I suspected that only a short time would elapse before the erosion would extend across the barrier beach road into the bay, creating a new inlet.

I awoke early on the morning of January 2, 1987, hearing the roar of the turbulent ocean from my home less than a mile away. An overnight storm had passed over the area, and I instinctively knew that the barrier beach had been breached in the area where the initial scouring took place several months before. I drove down to the beach with my video camera and recorded the historic event. Twenty-foot waves crashed across the barrier beach, sweeping directly into the bay on the other side, leveling and destroying a number of homes in their path.

Incredibly, during my near-death experience, less than three years before, I had watched a review of future events in my life that included this scene of destruction. Although I initially viewed this future vision as rather insignificant in the greater scheme of things, it was a significant confirmation to me that the future-event scenarios of my near-death experience were beginning to happen. What I realized quite significantly was that I instinctively and intuitively knew that the barrier beach was going to be breached in that particular location, and I knew when it was going to be breached.

The actuality of that event caused me to focus on another vivid vision that I had been shown of future storms that would affect this area of the barrier beach. During that vision, I had been shown a scene in which I was standing on a high clearing several miles from the ocean. From the clearing, I watched as a series of enormous tidal waves passed over the barrier beach. The massive waves picked up and destroyed all of the homes in their path, creating incredible flooding and destruction.

I realized that the clearing in this vision would have to be located in the elevated hills that traversed the eastern end of Long Island. These hills were part of the terminal moraine, a series of low-lying hills created during the Ice Age. I began to hike the trails in these hills in search of this clearing, somehow intuitively knowing that this site would have a significant place in future events in my life. I was even having vivid dreams of standing on this elevated clearing looking out over the panoramic view of the Atlantic Ocean to the south, when significant events were to take place. Unfortunately, I had miscalculated the location of this hillside clearing, perceiving it to be further to the east of its actual location, and it would be years before I would find it.

Over the next several years I slipped more comfortably back into my materialistic existence and no further future visions became part of my reality. During this time, I concentrated on my real estate business, opened two new offices, and developed a large staff of real estate salespeople. Ginnie managed the business affairs of Club Marakesh while I concentrated on my real estate business. This was a period in my life when I compartmentalized my past near-death and spiritual experiences and attempted to continue to focus my energies on my businesses. However, it had been years since I had any interest in remaining in the nightclub business, and I would have sold the nightclub if it were not for Ginnie's desire to remain in the business. It was this decision that kept us involved in each other's lives, years after our personal relationship had first ended.

In the summer of 1990, Ginnie informed me that she was pregnant and had decided to bring her child into the world as a single mother. I was taken by surprise but admired Ginnie for her courage and conviction. Later on, when Ginnie informed me that she was going to have a boy, I began to have recurrent visions of my near-death experience, when I had been shown the group of toddlers in the garden setting—particularly of the little boy with blonde hair. Those children were the children in spirit of the souls that were intended to be my children during my Earth life. They were the opportunities that I had decided were "inconveniences."

Although I was excited that Ginnie was going to have a boy, I was saddened myself when I realized years ago that I had passed over the opportunities that were presented to me to be a father. As Ginnie came closer to giving birth, I began to realize more fully the understanding that God had bestowed upon me during my near-death experience—the sanctity of life—a gift I never would have understood or appreciated without God's intervention in my life. During this time, I also began to reflect on my own childhood and how I had been deprived of a life with a father. Knowing that Ginnie was going to have a boy and remembering from my near-death experience that I was going to be given another opportunity to become the father of a little boy, I realized that my God-given opportunity was now at hand.

I was present in the delivery room when Michael came into this world. What an experience! Michael had blond hair that was almost golden and the biggest blue eyes I have ever seen on a little boy. I listened as the nurses marveled at how strong and developed his little body was. As I watched Michael being born and his strong little body struggling to stay alive as his soul breathed its first breath, I felt a radiance fill the delivery room. I felt a rush of wind roll by my ears carrying a message of love. It was a message I remembered hearing from a Lady of Light many years before: "Truly, he is a son of God!"

On the joyous day that Ginnie and Michael were released from Southampton Hospital, we drove to the town hall to file the certificate of birth. As Ginnie and I completed the forms, I was overcome with emotion when I realized that a "meaningful arrangement" had been created by the combination of our middle names. Ginnie's middle name is Mary. My middle name is Joseph, in honor of St. Joseph, the foster father of Jesus.

Before Michael was born, Ginnie and I had decided to have Michael's grandmothers recommend first and middle names. For my mother, we named Michael in honor of both the Archangel Michael and my stepfather Michael, who had died several years before. Michael's maternal grandmother chose Christopher for his middle name. The name Christopher means "Christ-bearing."

As I was filling out the forms, I realized that our combined middle names became Mary, Joseph, and Christopher. One may regard this combination as pure chance, but I don't believe so. I regard this meaningful arrangement as a wonderful message directed to me to validate again that what I experienced on the evening of July 2, 1984, was a real and true event in my life.

I could not possibly have anticipated that I was about to experience a series of significant and powerful spiritual experiences in the next several months. I should have recognized—possibly I did subconsciously recognize—that the future visions that were part of my near-death experience would not just go away. I should have realized that my recovery from alcoholism was a necessary prerequisite for me to be ready for the next stage of my mission in life—precipitated by what I call the mystical "phone call from heaven."

CHAPTER 21

PHONE CALL FROM HEAVEN

Meaningful coincidences are thinkable as pure
chance. But the more they multiply and the greater
and more exact the correspondence is, the more
their probability sinks and the unthinkability
increases, until they can no longer be regarded as
pure chance but, for lack of a causal explanation,
have to be thought of as meaningful arrangements.
—C. G. Jung

In the summer of 1994 I was drawn to drive north
from the village of Eastport near my Hamptons home
on a road I had not previously traveled. As I drove on the
winding two-lane road, passing farm lands rising
slightly above sea level, I sensed that I was heading in
the right direction to find the elusive clearing that had
been the object of my visions. The road began to wind
and snake up through the low-lying foothills into the
Pine Barren forest. Suddenly a sign appeared on the far
side of the road that caused me to brake abruptly. The

carved wooden sign read in bold letters, "Shrine of Our Lady of the Island."

I knew that my search for the clearing with the panoramic view of the ocean was nearly over. I made a left turn onto the roadway leading into the shrine property. I soon found a parking lot with a sign indicating a pathway to the outdoor shrine. I parked and walked up the winding footpath, looking for the highest elevation on the pine-forested property. I saw a clearing in the woods high above and with a panoramic view overlooking the plains of the Hamptons. In the distance, the barrier beach beyond the inland bays was spread out before me, and beyond was the Atlantic. This was the clearing that had been part of my NDE visions ten years before.

The clearing was several hundred feet above sea level, just as I had seen. It was the exact view of the land, inland bays, barrier beach, and ocean that I saw, then dreamed about, for years.

At the center of the clearing stood an enormous granite boulder. Almost square in shape, it rose fifteen feet out of the ground—weighing at least three hundred tons. Anchored to the top of the boulder, a granite statue rose another eighteen feet into the air, commanding a panoramic view of the ocean. Seeing the statue confirmed that my journey in search of the clearing was over. The statue was of the Lady of Light. I sensed that things were speeding up now, that events resulting from my near-death experience were going to multiply and have a considerably greater impact on my life.

I began to visit the shrine property and the statue of Our Lady of the Island frequently. I sensed that this sacred place had great significance in my journey. The property consisted of seventy acres of Pine Barren forest on sloping hills and was filled with trails through the woods, ideal for contemplative walks. One of the trails, the Way of the Cross, included the fourteen stations of the cross. This trail led to a high, sloping hillside that contained a lifelike scene of the hill of Calvary and the Crucifixion. Another trail began with a giant cross cut from evergreen bushes to mark the entrance to the Rosary Prayer Walk. One hundred and fifty juniper bushes, spaced in a quarter-mile circle, each represented an individual prayer, the Hail Mary. Each decade of ten Hail Marys represented a mystery in the life, death, passion, and glory of Jesus Christ and the life of Mary, His mother.

The shrine had been established by the Montfort Missionaries, a group of priests and brothers founded in France and inspired by the life and works of St. Louis Marie de Montfort (1673-1716). Montfort was recognized by the Catholic Church for his prophetic visions of the End Times, the period preceding the Second Coming of Christ.

The property for the shrine had been donated by Crescenzo and Angelina Vigliotta, farmers and landowners in Eastport, who had fifteen children, three of whom died in infancy. Their son, Bill, was in the seminary of the Montfort Missionaries in the 1950s when the land had been donated. When Father Bill visited the site, he discovered the monolith boulder during the clearing of an adjacent piece of property. The owners subsequently donated the boulder and the site to the Montfort Missionaries. Father Bill envisioned erecting the eighteen-foot statue upon the boulder, and he commissioned a sculptor, Rafael de Soto, to design it. The design was fashioned from a small wooden statue carved by St. Louis de Montfort himself, which uncharacteristically depicted Mary without a veil covering her head. Since St. Louis de Montfort's prophesies focused on the Second Coming of Christ, it is quite possible that the absence of the veil was symbolic of the lifting of the veil between the material and spiritual worlds that is prophesied to take place during the End Times.

The Lady of the Island statue had been carved at the Rock of Ages Quarry in Vermont, and it was delivered on a flatbed trailer truck to the Eastport shrine on September 10, 1975, then hoisted by crane atop the boulder. With a panoramic view of the Atlantic, the statue seems to be waiting for the fulfillment of the prophecies concerning the End Times.

On Sunday morning I returned to the shrine and received a mystical "phone call from heaven." Just over ten years had passed since my near-death experience. During those ten years, I was aware that I was going through a growing process dealing with the aftereffects of the experience, recovering from my alcoholism, and becoming increasingly aware that I was being prepared for my mission in life. Although my mission had been shown to me in a series of future visions, I was not sure how I was to integrate this mission into my life. The answers came to me in a most unusual and unexpected way on this Sunday morning at the shrine. It was a sunny and pleasant morning as I headed up the trail to the clearing at the top of the shrine. The Montfort Missionaries regularly held Sunday morning Mass at the outdoor shrine, but the Mass on this particular Sunday had been announced as a Healing Mass.

The celebrant of the Mass was a Capuchin priest, Father Peter McCall. When the Mass was over, people began to form lines on the lawn, and Father McCall and Maryann Lacy began to pray in front of each person. Then they placed anointing oils on their foreheads. With this, the people appeared to go into a trance, closing their eyes, falling backward and seeming to faint onto the lawn. Others would break their fall and pray over them as they lay on the ground.

I had seen this kind of performance before on TV evangelist shows, but I never expected to see this kind of healing at a Catholic ceremony. I watched as hundreds lined up and fell back as this priest and woman touched them. I had no intention of getting healed this way.

After thirty minutes of this ritual, maybe twenty people were still sitting in the last row. Suddenly, I felt as if I was picked up out of my seat by invisible forces grabbing my shoulders. Just as suddenly, I was standing at the end of the line, then Father McCall was in front of me. He grabbed me by the wrist to anoint my forehead. As he made contact with my forehead, I felt a burst of energy radiate from his touch and enter into me. The energy rushed through my body and exploded into a brilliant light in my head. My eyelids fluttered and my knees weakened as I, too, fell backwards onto the lawn. I felt as if I was back in the Light of God. I remained on the ground with my eyes closed, enveloped by this bright and loving light that filled my being.

I heard a woman's voice close to me, a voice that reminded me of the Lady of Light. Another woman joined her, and the two women began praying over me, one of them speaking in tongues, while the other woman spoke to me directly. "Have you ever been prayed over before? We have been inspired to pray over you! Is that okay?"

I nodded affirmatively without opening my eyes. I sensed that I was experiencing a powerful event. One woman continued to speak in a soft voice. "I was instructed to pray over you specifically. I don't know why I am receiving this message. I am being told to speak to your heart, to your spirit, and this is the message: 'Ned, you have been wrestling inwardly for a long time now. You have known for a long time now that you have a decision to make. You have known for a long time what you have to do. Now it is time.' "

Simultaneously, I was hearing the same message from an interior voice as if it was coming directly from the Lady of Light. The message was loud and clear, and it triggered an immediate response from deep inside me.

It was clear to me what the meaning of the message was. For several months, I had been drawn to this shrine knowing that I was going to receive a message related to the visions and messages of my near-death experience. I had known for a long time that I had been sent back from my near-death experience with a mission. I was not sure when that mission was to begin or how I was going to accomplish it. However, now that I had received this "phone call from heaven," I knew that it was time.

The sun was shining brilliantly as I opened my eyes. I had trouble focusing at first. I was intent on finding the woman who had given me the message, but I had no idea who she was. There were a number of men and women assisting Father McCall and Maryann Lacy, but I had no way of identifying this mysterious woman. As I regained my composure, I realized that I had undergone a transformation during the healing process. For the past several months, I had an inner sense that things were going to "speed up." It had been ten years since my near-death experience, and it was time for me to begin to process the visions and messages I had received during it. I had learned early on that the near-death visions were to take place when they were meant to take place, and that I could not accelerate the process. I instinctively knew that the process was "speeding up"; it was the "phone call from heaven" that confirmed it.

CHAPTER 22

ACCEPTANCE

I returned home from the shrine recognizing that I had a new agenda to follow. Previously, I had been devoting most of my time to my business interests. I realized now that I would have to step back from these and focus on my mission. I would have to risk a loss of income or possibly even lose some of my business interests, but I was unconcerned. I had spent the last ten years focusing on business, but part of me knew that the sense of mission would not go away, and it was more important than anything else. It was time for me to start my mission, just as I had been shown I would during my NDE ten years earlier.

I would conduct research concerning my NDE, and write about it. I wanted my research and writing to be as credible and valid as possible. The first obstacle was that I had to be dragged to my desk just to write a short business letter. How was I going to write and do research, or discipline myself to become a scholar of mystical experiences?

I needed some time to get away and think about the direction that my life was taking. Paul, my friend and

AA sponsor, was planning to drive to his home in Florida on the day following the healing service, but he sprained his ankle and couldn't drive. I decided to drive his car to Florida for him. On the first evening of the drive, we arrived in Virginia Beach and passed the campus of the Association for Research and Enlightenment (ARE). I did not know why I had been drawn to this place but I decided that the next morning I would visit the campus.

At the ARE reception area, while asking the receptionist for information, I noticed a poster for a conference called "Life Everlasting! . . . The Near Death Experience!" I knew that I was meant to attend that conference.

At the conference one month later, I heard seminars by Dr. Raymond Moody, author of *Life After Life,* and Dannion Brinkley, author of *Saved By the Light.* In 1975, Dannion had been talking on the telephone when he was struck by lightning. He had been thrown several feet into the air, his heart stopped, and he was clinically dead for twenty-eight minutes. During that time, he had a near-death experience in which "Beings of Light" showed him 117 future events, including the Chernobyl nuclear disaster, the Persian Gulf War, and America's future economic crisis.

As I was exiting an elevator in the conference hotel lobby on the day the conference ended, I noticed Dannion Brinkley standing in the lobby with his back to me. He immediately turned around and pointed straight at me. "We have to talk. Don't we?" he proclaimed. The amazing part of his statement was that he had read my thoughts as I was leaving the elevator. He continued, "What are you doing now? I'm starved. Let's have lunch."

Although we talked "normally" during lunch, the psychic connection that we retained from our separate near-death experiences provided an additional level of communication. Dannion sensed correctly that I was at a point in my life where I was about to go through a transition. Some near-death experiencers, like Dannion, returned from their NDE with an immediate sense of mission. Others, like myself, might experience ten or twenty years of processing the experience before reaching a point of awareness, or somehow being re-introduced to the Light and being driven by a sense of mission. Dannion, like many NDEers, had been drawn to hospice work.

Hospice provides an opportunity for the terminally ill to die with dignity. It gives palliative care and attends to the emotional, spiritual, social, and financial needs of the terminally ill patient at an inpatient facility or at the patient's home. Dannion realized that he had a gift to help people face the transition of death and that part of his mission was to offer comfort to the dying by help-ing them lose their fear of death through understanding how we make the transition through death. Dannion and I discussed hospice and other near-death related issues over a lunch that lasted three and one-half hours.

Although I had not trained through a hospice organization at the time, I shared Dannion's interest in speaking about the near-death experience with other people who were facing death. On a number of occa-sions, I had shared my experience with friends and loved ones who were facing death.

The first time was with my aunt who had been sud-denly hospitalized with terminal cancer. The day before she died, I visited her bedside alone and while holding her hand told her about my NDE. She was very close to death at the time, but she acknowledged her under-standing and appreciation by squeezing my hand as I told my story. I finished by telling my aunt that she should watch for the Light of God and go toward it when she was ready. My aunt responded, "I'm so glad you told me that. I was having these dreams, more like visions during the night. What you just told me makes everything clear to me now. I'm not afraid now. I'm ready to go."

My aunt's pre-death experience was typical of the process of death for those who die slowly. During the last hours, days, or even months before death, the dying may make statements or communicate in other ways that at first may be confusing for their families, friends, and health care workers. In reality, it is usually the onlookers who are confused by the dying person's demeanor, while the dying person is experiencing an orientation process to enable him or her to make the transition through death.

The experiences of those who are dying is similar to the experiences of near-death survivors. Dying people will speak of having visions of a place of peace and tranquility. They will often claim to see deceased friends and loved ones and/or religious figures. Sometimes the dying communicate that they know when they will die, or they appear to delay the time of their passing until certain circumstances are met. The dying usually experience (and are drawn to) a bright and radiant light that is visible only to them at the time of death.

I continued to visit the shrine frequently while I was conducting my NDE research. I was still intrigued by the identity of the woman who had given me the messages during the "phone call from heaven," but I believed that she was part of Father McCall's prayer group. Walking along a path at the Shrine one day I noticed a woman with a radiance, a certain charisma. The other women around her seemed to be drawn to her as she spoke. I introduced myself to one of the women and inquired about this charismatic woman whom I believed was the one who had prayed over me and had given me the message. The woman responded that the charismatic woman was Rose, a gifted visionary, who received inner locutions or heavenly messages from the Virgin Mary. When Rose noticed me, she smiled, walked over to me, and was about to introduce herself, when I interrupted her.

"How did you know my name?" I blurted out. "And where did you get that message for me from?"

"I was inspired to give you that message. It's hard to explain. During healing services, I receive messages to lay hands on specific people, many of whom I do not know. You were the second or third person I was told to pray over. I was told to go over to a gentleman who was suffering and in some kind of turmoil, and it turned out to be you."

"Well, your message was quite appropriate," I responded. "I had a near-death experience ten years ago, and your message was a confirmation of that experience."

"You had a near-death experience? Well, I did also," Rose added, "three years ago. As a result of my near-death experience, I have been given this gift. I was not particularly religious when I had the experience, but it changed my life. Now I come here often. I felt that I was called here after I had the experience. I use the word 'called,' because it is the only way I know to explain it. There are many other people who have started coming here recently, and they all say the same thing. They believe they have been 'called' here. A prayer group has been formed by the people who are 'called.' Each goes his or her separate way, but they are always drawn back to the shrine."

I had to interrupt her. "Now that you mention it, I felt that I was drawn here! I cannot explain it, but I felt this inner calling which drew me to this shrine.

Somehow it is related to visions that I had during my near-death experience, visions that are to take place in the future, and I believe these events will take place here at the shrine."

I had struck a chord. "You have had future visions of this place? I have also." We began to discuss our individual visions concerning the shrine, and some of our visions were similar. We both had visions that many more people would make pilgrimages to the shrine from places all over the world. In some cases, we were able to confirm each other's visions from different perspectives, even details that seemed to be insignificant. I described a vision of a future event at the shrine in which multitudes of people would converge at the shrine during the night. Rose had a similar vision.

"From overhead, I saw thousands of people carrying tiny lights on the roads and trails leading up to the shrine," she exclaimed, "and I saw fire engines parked along the road, but there was no fire, so I didn't understand why they would be there."

"The people you saw in the vision were carrying lit candles," I replied. "The fire engines would be there to safeguard against anyone accidentally starting a forest fire."

Rose and I discussed the fact that the Montfort Missionaries were continually expanding the shrine's facilities far beyond what was needed to accommodate its current visitors. They were obviously anticipating the future. Both Rose and I had visions that the expansion would be necessary due to the large number of people in the future.

It is significant that Rose and I were "drawn" or "called" to the Eastport shrine as a result of having near-death experiences and that Rose was given messages for me at a time when I was drawn to the shrine in search of answers. Of greater significance is the fact that I had visions indicating that future events at the shrine would foreshadow the End Times and that the shrine would become a safe place or haven for many people who would be drawn to the shrine during the End Times.

By late November, I was progressing in detailing the events of my NDE. On the days that I was inspired to write, I would usually awake before dawn and immediately begin to write. The writing seemed to come to me automatically—totally by inspiration. As my writing continued, I became more curious about the source of my inspirational writing, and I began to question the process within my own mind.

On Thanksgiving evening, my curiosity concerning the source of my inspiration was resolved for me. I was sitting at home writing, when I was abruptly brought to my senses by a powerful spiritual presence that appeared in the room. I looked up and saw a brilliant aura. A brilliant field of energy extended from several feet above the floor almost to the fourteen-foot high ceiling. The aura was not visibly manifested to the point that I could observe its source, but I recognized that my visitor was the Lady of Light.

I was enveloped by her aura. I viewed scenes, as if in a movie, of additional future events that were to take place at the Eastport shrine. The scenes were so real, so detailed, that I felt that I had been teleported into the future, experiencing these future events as if they were taking place now. I was initially confused because I thought I was being shown a single series of events that were to take place on a particular date. However, as the scenes continued to unfold, I realized that I was being shown future events that were to take place over a considerable period of time. These were similar to the visions I remembered from my NDE but with much more detail.

The next morning, I drove to the shrine at dawn. The scenes that I had been shown during the previous evening remained vividly with me. I wanted to find locations that were part of the future scenes. I walked up toward the top of the hill. As I reached the clearing, I saw the eastern end of Long Island in the distance, but I was drawn to an area next to the statue, to a large pine tree. I was drawn to this tree because I sensed the presence of the Lady of Light. As I knelt at the base of the tree, I was enveloped in a different time and space. I began to view the same visions I had seen the night before.

As the scenes ended, I sensed the Lady of Light even more strongly. She began to speak to me concerning my mission while reviewing scenes from my NDE. She showed me how the visions from my NDE were related to the visions I was now experiencing, and what I was expected to do to perform my mission. Then the visions ended, and the Lady of Light was gone.

I was inspired by the spiritual visitations of November and by my ten years of sobriety to continue my writing and research. However, in typical alcoholic fashion, I wanted more: more support, more inspiration, more validation that my spiritual path was not just the product of an overactive imagination.

I had had many spiritually validating experiences over the years. Some were subtle, others intense. I am by nature cynical and disbelieving, not content with accepting the reality of the visitations of November because I wanted a *physical* manifestation, a *physical* presence; certainty that what I was experiencing was real. I began to apply the same reality check to these visitations that I had applied to my near-death experience.

I wanted to be certain about the source of my inspiration and my writing. Just as I could not deny that the near-death experience was a real and true event, I wanted to be certain that the visionary experiences were real and true.

This confirmation finally came to me. On the morning of December 8, 1994, I went to the outdoor shrine at Eastport to pray and meditate. I meditated on my experiences, particularly those since the "phone call from heaven." There was no question that a number of significant mystical experiences were now occurring to me on a regular basis. These events were a confirmation that the future visions that had been shown to me during my near-death experience were now becoming a reality. I was being guided by inspiration and interior locutions. But I was still concerned that the path I was on was of my own making. Frankly, my life had become very comfortable. I felt that I was taking risks with my comfort as well as my sanity by embarking on the mystical path.

I began to pray on my knees for more than just a voice from heaven. I was communicating to God, to the Lady of Light, to the angels and saints, to anyone from above to come down and tap me on the shoulder and say to me, eye to eye, that I was on the right path. I was like a child demanding to be acknowledged. I spent an hour in this position as if I were trying to make a long distance overseas call and not getting through.

It had been a bright day, but after an hour a crisp December chill began to blow across the clearing. I didn't feel the presence of the spiritual as I had on the morning of November 25. I was frustrated and in despair as I decided to leave. I was thinking that I should put this stuff behind me. As I walked along the descending path, a flash of light emanated from the pine tree at the top of the clearing. At first, it seemed as if the pine tree was enveloped by a flash fire, but then the flash of fire moved away from the tree and formed an oval shape six feet high, and it came down the hillside and onto the path directly in front of me. I stood mesmerized as I realized that the golden flame came from a celestial being.

The light slowly moved forward up the pathway, several inches above the ground; I was motionless, marveling at the sight before me, as the Lady of Light paused in front of me. The radiant golden light seemed brighter than the Sun, but it did not burn or blind me. Rather, the light filled me with joy. Only moments before, I had been nurturing negative feelings and despair. Fortunately, those thoughts had been fleeting, for I was now getting the validation that I had almost demanded. The Lady of Light smiled at me as she read my thoughts. Then she spoke. "Now, everything that you have asked for has been given."

Then she was gone. The cloud of flame that surrounded her rose directly up into the sky until it was no longer visible. I stood glued to the spot. I conducted a reality check on myself. This visitation was not a hallucination. I was certain it was a real experience.

I walked slowly down the path, looking into the sky and in every direction in anticipation of her possible return. I was also looking for witnesses who may have viewed the extraordinary scene. But I had been alone at the top of the hill, and there were no other people along the path. Then, as I observed the tops of the trees along the path, clouds of golden light settled on the tops of the pine trees turning the branches and pine needles a deep violet.

At first, I thought the brilliant lights were flashpoints from the aftermath of the visitation by the Lady of Light, or that they were optical illusions, such as one would experience following the intense light of a camera's flash or from momentarily being blinded by the Sun. But the brilliant clouds of light were only settling on the trees around me as I walked. As soon as I moved along the path, each of the clouds of light would rise from its treetop and move further down the path, settling on the top of another tree directly in front of me—as if they were all leading and following me along the path. As I kept walking slowly down the path, the clouds of light rose from the trees I had just passed and then settled on the treetops in front of me. It became a game for me. I would walk ten paces, stop abruptly, and then turn around while watching the bright clouds of light settle only on the trees surrounding me, as if they were a flock of birds and I was carrying their feed.

I perceived that the clouds of light were independent and intelligent beings manifesting as beams of light. This was not a hallucination, or an optical illusion, or a defect of sight. I was experiencing a communication from another realm of existence, from a spiritual realm. The Lady of Light had left her "calling cards," a flock of angels that surrounded me during my walk. The angels, manifesting as bright clouds of light, were a confirmation of the validity of the Lady of Light's visitation.

When I reached the shrine's main roadway the apparitions ceased, but I was still in awe of what I had just experienced. I retreated to the solitude of a chapel and sat in a pew contemplating the visitation. It was during this period of contemplative meditation that I heard the voice of the Lady of Light through an interior locution. In a clear voice, she said: "Go to Egypt!"

It was a simple message, specific and to the point. I was told to go to Egypt. But why? I had no reason to go to Egypt, nor could I imagine why going halfway across the world to Egypt would have any bearing on my spiritual journey. However, the message was so clear that I could not overlook it or attempt to rationalize the message as some sort of auditory hallucination.

I returned to my Hamptons home that morning and sat down at the kitchen table, exhausted from my experiences at the shrine. I began nonchalantly leafing through a pile of mostly unwanted mail when my fingers suddenly froze on a particular envelope. It was a moment in my life that Carl Jung would have described as a "meaningful coincidence," one that is unthinkable as pure chance.

The piece of mail was an invitation to join a group on an archaeological expedition to the ancient ruins of Egypt. The trip was scheduled for late February and March, only months away. As I read the trip's itinerary, I still could not fathom the significance of my being told to go to Egypt until I read the itinerary for the final day of the trip: "We will visit the site of the apparitions of the Blessed Virgin Mary at the Coptic Orthodox Church of St. Mary in Zeitoun, Cairo."

I did not hesitate. I picked up the phone and dialed the "800" number to make my reservation. I was going to Egypt.

CHAPTER 23

TRIP TO EGYPT

February 28-March 10, 1995

> She became known to me as the Lady of Light, and
> she radiated an incredibly golden light far brighter
> and of a much greater magnitude than the light of
> any of the other angelic or spiritual beings. Clearly,
> the Lady of Light held a very high place in the spir-
> itual hierarchy of this heavenly realm.
>
> *—Notes from my near-death experience.*

On the evening of February 28, I boarded Egypt Air
Flight 988 and settled into my window seat, awake and
alert in anticipation of the trip to Cairo. I had had no
previous desire, motivation, or reason to go to Egypt. My
decision to go was based solely on faith—a belief and
trust that the Lady of Light wanted me to make this
pilgrimage. I was so convinced that there was a divine
purpose behind this trip that I fell asleep easily and

didn't wake until the next morning when the plane was on its final approach to Cairo.

We landed on the busiest day of the year for Egypt, the final day, the final hour of Ramadan, Islam's month-long fast. There was more than the usual chaos and confusion at the airport. After clearing customs, I met with other members of the tour group and with the group's guide, Ahmed Fayed. We boarded buses that took us to the Mena House Hotel from which I could see the Great Pyramid complex.

For several days, we toured the ancient sites near Cairo, including the Great Pyramids, Sphinx, and Step Pyramids at Saqqâra. We then flew to Luxor and visited ancient Karnak, the temples at Luxor, and the Valley of the Kings, where we visited the tombs of King Tutankhamen, Ramses, and other great pharaohs. We then boarded a cruise ship and sailed for several days up the Nile, visiting the Idfu and Kom-Ombo temples and other sites, ending in Aswan where we flew back to Cairo.

On the final day, we traveled for several hours by bus through the clogged and narrow streets of Cairo to visit the Marian apparition site in Zeitoun. I sensed that the apparition site was the reason I had been instructed to go to Egypt. I was not familiar with, nor did I seek out, what had happened at Zeitoun. During the bus ride Ahmed Fayed told me about the apparitions.

The apparitions at Zeitoun were seen by crowds of up to 250,000 Christians, Jews, and Muslims from 1968 until 1971. If what he said was true, the apparitions at Zeitoun were an incredible validation of the existence of the spiritual world. Yet, apparently the Western world has ignored the occurrences at Zeitoun. As a Roman Catholic student at St. Gabriel's High School, I had been familiar with the Marian apparitions at Lourdes, France, and Fátima, Portugal. At Lourdes in 1858, French schoolgirl Bernadette Soubirous, age fourteen, claimed to have had eighteen visions over a six-month period of "a lady" dressed in a white robe. At Fátima in 1917, three children claimed to have experienced similar visions. Although the Roman Catholic Church eventually approved these apparition sites due to the documentation of miraculous cures as well as religious conversions, the apparitions of the Virgin Mary were seen by only a few.

It is believed that the Holy Family traveled through the Zeitoun area 2,000 years ago during their flight to Egypt to avoid Herod's edict to massacre the newly-born male children in Israel. A Christian sect, called Copts, survives to this day, mostly in Egypt. When the bus arrived in Zeitoun at St. Mary's Coptic Church, I was startled at how small the church appeared. It was charming, made of stucco with a large dome at the top and a smaller dome over each of the corners. It was above and around these domes that the visions of a Lady of Light first appeared on the evening of April 2, 1968. After viewing the church, I sat down in a shady spot to read about one of the more astounding manifestations of the spiritual world in our time. The following account describes what happened in Zeitoun on that evening:

A cool, gentle breeze blew through the narrow streets of Zeitoun, lifting away the dusty heat that the burning sun had delivered to the Cairo suburb during the day. Earthly doves do not fly by night, but on this quiet night spiritual doves of light circled Zeitoun from a high vantage point in the starlit sky. In formation, the doves of light continued their flight down over cramped buildings teeming with humanity, and above and over the silent streets. Seven of these doves of light, in a formation suggestive of a cross, flew down and over Tumanbay Street, the main thoroughfare of Zeitoun. As the doves moved over the street, they appeared as luminous objects, round and golden in color. They could be seen clearly by any of the observers from the street below; the wings of each appeared to be motionless and fixed in flight.

The seven doves continued their flight along Tumanbay in their cross formation until they reached the corner of Khalil Lane, where Saint Mary's Coptic Church stands. Above the intersection of Tumanbay and Khalil, the doves hovered momentarily, broke formation, and moved to seven different locations above the highest dome of St. Mary's. The doves of light seemed to float down and settle in the night sky surrounding the domes of the church. Then they vanished into the darkness of the night, barely noticed by the few pedestrians along Khalil Lane.

Khalil Lane had been named after the family of Khalil Ibrahim, a devout Egyptian Copt. In 1918, when Zeitoun was still a desert area on the edge of Cairo, one very wealthy member of the Khalil Ibrahim family suffered a family crisis. During the night, a Lady of Light appeared to him in a vision and told him to build a Coptic church on the land in her honor. If he built the church, she told him, she would return in fifty years (1968) and bless the church with her presence. Soon after, the Khalil Ibrahim family arranged for the construction of the church. It was opened in 1925 and was named St. Mary's in honor of the Lady of Light.

During the day, Zeitoun was usually a bustling and crowded suburb, but on this particular evening, Tumanbay Street had little traffic. Khalil Lane was practically deserted, except during the 8:30 P.M. change of shifts at the public transportation system garage across the street from the church. Farouk Mohammed Atwa, a Muslim worker, had just finished his day shift and sat with a group of co-workers at the gates of the garage building, attempting to enjoy his mug of tea. He was momentarily distracted by what appeared in his peripheral vision—meteors or shooting stars in the sky above the domes of St. Mary's. However, Farouk was distracted only for an instant and made no comment on the sight; such appearances were not so unusual in the brilliant night sky above Cairo.

Besides, Farouk had to contend with the throbbing pain that emanated from the heavily bandaged forefinger of his right hand. Normally, at day's end his customary mug of tea offered him comfort and peace. But as he sipped the tea, it offered him little solace from the pain and discomfort of his damaged finger. He was scheduled to be admitted into the hospital the following morning to have his finger surgically amputated to prevent the continuing spread of gangrene.

The first sign that anything unusual was about to happen came from a flurry of alarmed whisperings among several women who were standing in the middle of the lamplit street. At that moment, Farouk looked up at what appeared to be a young lady, enveloped in light, kneeling at the cross on the top of the dome. Convinced that the young woman was about to commit suicide, Farouk ran into the street while pointing up to the dome with his heavily bandaged forefinger. "Lady, don't jump! Don't jump!" he shouted repeatedly. "Lady! Don't jump!"

It then occurred to Farouk that it was not humanly possible for a young girl to kneel on the rounded surface of the dome, but the girl appeared to be supported and surrounded by a strange, glowing, and golden light. At that moment, the lady seemed to respond to Farouk's warning by rising to her feet. Farouk now saw a beautiful and magnificent spirit dressed in luminous and shimmering robes of light.

Disbelieving his eyes but recognizing an emergency situation, Farouk ran into the transportation building to call the rescue squad. Several of his co-workers ran in the other direction to the church residence to get help. After calling for help, Farouk returned with other workers to Khalil Lane. His other co-workers also returned from the church residence, accompanied by St. Mary's pastor, Father Constantine. Khalil Lane was now crowded with onlookers who were pointing to the rooftop of St. Mary's, each of them attempting to comprehend the luminous apparition of the Lady of Light.

One woman in the street began to cry out, "*Settena Mariam! Settena Mariam!*" Farouk stood in the middle of the street, stupefied, engrossed in the luminous spectacle. However, he was consciously aware that something strange seemed to be happening to him as the pain from his injured hand seemed to diminish. Temporarily stunned by the mesmerizing sight above St. Mary's Church dome, Farouk observed that his gangrenous finger, which he had pointed to the Lady of Light, was suddenly and miraculously healed and free of gangrene.

Just then, shouts of joy went up from the assembled crowd as a flight of glowing white doves appeared in the sky above the dome and floated down in a protective circle surrounding the luminous body of light. As the women in the street continued to shout, "*Settena Mariam! Settena Mariam!*" the luminous Lady of Light, surrounded by the celestial doves, floated into the brilliant star-filled sky and disappeared into the night.

Approximately one month following the first apparition in April 1968, an investigative committee of twelve bearded and black-robed Coptic bishops and clergymen held a press conference at the patriarchal palace in Cairo. They had been appointed by Pope Kyrillos VI, the Pope of Alexandria, Egypt, and the Coptic Orthodox Patriarch, to investigate the apparitions at Zeitoun and to report their findings to him. The church's investigators concluded:

We have the great honor to submit to your Holiness (Pope Kyrillos VI) these investigations regarding the appearances of the Blessed Virgin's apparitions in our Coptic Orthodox Church in Zeitoun, Cairo. On April 23, 1968, after being delegated by your Holiness, we went to the spot where the church is located and started to get in touch with those who had observed the apparitions.

Upon summarizing the reports of the garage workmen, we have come to the conclusion that the apparition of the Blessed Virgin Mary has appeared several times on and in the domes of the church since April 2, 1968. The appearances have mostly been observed by the workmen of the garage whose witness has been confirmed by the inhabitants of Zeitoun, both Muslims and Christians. Multitudes of people from different parts of the country have all watched the apparitions of the Blessed Virgin and a great number of them have certified the certainty of the appearances, sending their testimony with enthusiastic written messages.

We then determined to witness the blessed apparitions with our own eyes in order to have the matter cleared up plainly and evidently. We stayed opposite the domes, watching some nights until we could see the Blessed Virgin Mary appearing inside a luminous circle. Then she appeared in her complete form, moving on the domes, and then bowing before the cross, and at the end she blessed the multitudes. Another night, we saw doves with the bright color of silver and with light radiating from them. The doves flew from the dome and into the sky. We then glorified Almighty God who has allowed the terrestrials to see the glory of the celestials.

I paused from my reading and viewed the small church from my shady spot, but my thoughts were on my own experience 5,600 miles away at the Eastport shrine. The accounts of the Zeitoun apparitions reminded me of my experience at the shrine, and the doves of light that accompanied the apparitions of Mary were very similar to the "clouds of light" that I saw settling on the treetops "like a flock of birds."

The official report concerning the apparitions had been released at the news conference along with an official statement from Pope Kyrillos, which added:

The appearances have been witnessed by many thousands of citizens and foreigners belonging to different religions and sects, together with groups of religious organizations and scientific and professional personages and all other categories of people, who have proclaimed and announced their witnesses, confirming the certainty of the Virgin's appearances—all giving the same particulars as to description and form and time and place, thus proving a whole agreement in witnessing that has elevated the matter of appearance above any doubt or any lack of proof or evidence.

To my knowledge, never before in the history or study of supernatural phenomena had convincing photographic evidence ever been produced as evidence of a supernatural visitation. But many photographs of the apparitions at Zeitoun were taken, documenting the apparitions. They do exist, and were taken by many different individuals, including a photographer for Egypt's semi-official newspaper *Al Ahram*. Most of the photos taken showed only a burst of light or the shape of a figure within the light. However, the photos were accompanied by written accounts describing the details that the witnesses had observed. Some of the photos were more detailed, clearly showing the image of Mary. Many of the photos even captured the doves of light.

The investigative committee's report and the official statement of Pope Kyrillos VI created front page headlines in all six of Cairo's newspapers, which included articles and actual photographs of the celestial apparitions. The news of the apparitions was widely covered throughout the Middle East but, incredibly, only a few foreign or overseas newspapers gave any notice to the events in Zeitoun.

Thomas F. Brady, a special correspondent to the *New York Times*, attended the news conference and wrote a short article appearing in the *New York Times* on Sunday, May 5, 1968. Although the *Times* article dealt primarily with the official news release, it also mentioned that "the first report of appearances came April 2 when, according to press accounts, a Muslim garage keeper awoke a priest of the Church of the Virgin to tell him that there was a woman on the church's roof, apparently bent on suicide."

A subsequent news article in the *New York Times* on August 11, 1968, overlooked the fact that thousands of Christians, Muslims, Jews, and unbelievers were by then making pilgrimages to Zeitoun. On certain evenings, as many as 250,000 observers had filled the narrow streets of the Cairo suburb and witnessed the apparitions. The article focused on a curious but noteworthy episode. A young Coptic priest, Father Youhanna Boulos, with a silver cross in his hand, was observed by the *Times* reporter attempting to exorcise an epileptic man named Mohammed Ahmed Abbassy, who was sprawled on a Muslim prayer sheet in the churchyard. The young priest commented: "With the help of the Virgin, it is easy to draw the devils out."

Many names have been ascribed to the Lady of Light. She is most simply addressed as Mary, Mother of God. She has been named for the many locations throughout the world where she has been known to appear: Our Lady of: Betania, Fátima, Guadeloupe, Knock, La Salette, Lourdes, Medjugorje, and Zeitoun. She has been highly honored by Roman Catholics, Orthodox, Anglican, and Christian sects who profess a belief in her perpetual virginity, hence the names the Virgin, the Blessed Virgin Mary. In 1854, the Vatican proclaimed the dogma of the Immaculate Conception, which states that Mary was conceived and born without original sin. Among all of God's creatures, she stands alone graced by God with special gifts; hence she is known as the Queen of Heaven, Queen of the Angels, Queen of the Universe. Her messages of love and healing are dispensed to all of humanity, as evidenced most convincingly by some of her appearances in Zeitoun when she appeared to be holding out an olive branch to Christians, Muslims, Jews, and unbelievers. Many Islamic traditions recognize the virgin birth of the prophet Jesus Christ, and hold that Mary was conceived without original sin, so she is venerated in Muslim devotions.

During my near-death experience, she became known to me as the Lady of Light. Whenever I would recall the experience or be reminded of her intercession in my life, I would always think of her as the Lady of Light, yet I had never heard any reference to her from any other source as the Lady of Light—that is, until I visited Zeitoun.

Prior to her appearances in Egypt, the Coptic Church had designated thirty-one feast days on the church calendar to specifically honor Mary. The thirty-second feast day was added on April 2, 1969, the first anniversary of her appearances in Zeitoun. The Coptic Church decided to name that day in her honor as the Feast Day of Our Lady of Light.

I recognized why I had come all these miles to this small church in Egypt. Even after my experiences of apparitions at the Eastport shrine, I was still by nature cynical and disbelieving. I wanted to be certain that the visionary experiences were real and true. From everything I read about the Zeitoun apparitions, and after observing the photographs of the apparitions, I realized that the Lady of Light's visits to Zeitoun confirmed for me that my experiences at the Eastport shrine were real and true events in my life.

As I crossed the street and entered St. Mary's Church, my breath was taken away by a life-size portrait that hung in the entrance of the Church. The artist had captured what the photographs could not: a portrait of the Lady of Light as she had appeared at St. Mary's Church in Zeitoun, and just as she had appeared to me at Our Lady of the Island Shrine in Eastport, New York, on the morning of December 8, 1994.

CHAPTER 24

ATTEMPTING TO PLAN
THE FUTURE

When I returned from Egypt, I implemented a strategy designed to permit me to make a complete transition from the life I had been leading to a more spiritual path according to what the future visions foretold. First, I aggressively marketed the sale of both my real estate businesses and the nightclub. I knew I had to completely break my ties with my business interests, particularly with Club Marakesh. I also put my home on the market with great sadness; I loved my home in which I had lived for almost twenty years, and did not want to sell it. But I had been shown during my NDE that my spiritual mission in life would not begin until I divested myself of my past life, including my material possessions, particularly my businesses and my Hamptons home. I knew that I would be traveling extensively in the future and that I would eventually settle in the mountain and valley area shown to me in the future visions, in the area known to me as "Sugarloaf."

By April 1996 I had a deal negotiated on Club Marakesh and was close to another deal on the real estate business. Since 1984, I had been living with the foreknowledge that I was going to lose all of my material possessions before I embarked on a more spiritual path in my life. Now I was planning for the loss of my possessions by divesting myself of the things I knew I was going to lose, and in return, profiting from divesting myself of these things in a way that would assure me financial security and a passive income well into the future. I allowed myself to believe that everything was going to go my way just as I had planned.

Even though I still owned the businesses, I was spending more time doing hospice work and volunteering at the shrine. For instance, I spent April 6, 1995, as a volunteer assisting the Montfort Missionaries in providing services for the thousands of worshippers who converged on the shrine for Good Friday devotions. As a volunteer, I did the same kind of "grunt" work that I normally hired other people to do as a nightclub owner: cleaning the bathrooms; taking out the garbage; directing traffic in the parking lots. It was humbling but rewarding work. I didn't see a Mercedes-Benz, BMW, or Porsche all day long; nor did I see anyone I recognized from the Hamptons and most certainly no one from Palm Beach.

The visitors to the shrine came from countries all over the world and from every religion. In my days as an arrogant nightclub owner, I doubt that I would have chosen any of these people to get beyond the velvet ropes and into my nightclubs. But then I had never experienced the kind of bonding in all my years as a nightclub owner that I did on this special day at the Eastport shrine. My experiences at the shrine that day were a validation that each and every life is just as important and significant as every other and that any one single life is not more important than any other. I made certain that I extended a smile of greeting to as many people as I met during the day.

Although it was a cold, damp day, the spirits of the worshippers were not dampened as they gathered in prayer at the grottos or along the shrine's many paths. However, a steady downpour of sleet and rain during the afternoon drew the crowds to the warmth of the shrine's buildings. I walked up the trail to "The Rock," as the clearing at the top of the hill was called. A small group was huddled under a canopy there. I recognized the leader of the group as a visionary from the Philippines, a young man who received messages from heaven. Many of the messages he received while living in the Philippines forewarned of cataclysmic events that were to happen in the United States in the not-too-distant future.

Many visionaries had been inexplicably drawn to the Eastport shrine in the past year. I was not surprised. St. Louis de Montfort, who inspired the founding of the Montfort Missionaries and the Eastport shrine, prophetically wrote about "the apostles of the End Time . . . chosen souls, a mighty legion of brave and valiant soldiers . . . both men and women" who would be drawn to assist the Montfort Missionaries in the realization of God's plan during the End Times. All of the visionaries who were drawn to the shrine agreed that we were already experiencing the End Times.

As the early evening faded into dusk, I stood alone at the clearing at the top of the shrine. The crowds had gone for the day, and I was the only person left on the seventy-acre shrine grounds. A twinkling of lights began to appear on the plains of the Hamptons. On the horizon directly to the south is the fragile strip of sand that formed the barrier beach. From my vantage point, I could clearly see that the barrier beach was now devoid of over one hundred and fifty homes that were swept out to sea by the rising tides and increasing number of storms since 1987. It was easy to see from this clearing how another storm could easily devastate the entire shoreline, as I was shown would happen in the future.

The clearing at the top of the shrine was quiet but in the distance there was the whine of tires and a steady stream of headlights leading to the Hamptons, a procession of Mercedes-Benzes, BMWs, and Porsches fleeing Manhattan for the weekend.

As I watched, I knew the cellular car phones were probably clogging the airwaves as the Hamptons-bound travelers made their weekend plans. It was the beginning of the spring season in the Hamptons, a time to tune up for the summer. In the trendy restaurants and clubs preparing for the night's business, the Dom Perignon, Cristal, and Perrier Jouet would be chilling in preparation for the affluent crowd. Maître d's would be anxious, hoping to draw the "right crowd" for the summer. A trendy Hamptons night spot could live or die based on its ability to attract the year's latest "hot crowd" of celebrities, sports personalities, and young models.

As I continued to watch the Good Friday evening turn to night, I began to take inventory of where my life was heading. I realized that I would not be joining the "right crowd" that evening. Once there was a time in my life when being part of the hot crowd was the essence of my existence. At first, being part of the in crowd was exhilarating, then I became numbed by the superficiality of the scene, and finally it became painful to be part of it. Somehow, I had lost interest in the mundane rites of passage, quite suddenly in fact, on the evening of July 2, 1984. On the whole, I preferred to spend the evening alone on top of the clearing looking up at the stars, and dreaming about "home."

As night fell over the plains of the Hamptons, I was mesmerized by the twinkling of lights, which seemed to magically blend along the horizon with the stars as the day's storm clouds dissolved in the night sky. In the skies above me, I could visualize my spiritual home to which I shall return when my earthly journey is over. In the distance below me, I could see the location of my earthly home in the Hamptons. I had learned to become comfortable with my earthly home since my near-death experience. I had learned peace and serenity as a result of my experience. Most importantly, I had learned that I no longer fear death. I knew that my existence on Earth is transitory. Even the Earth itself is transitory. At one time in the past, the Earth did not exist. At some point in the future, it will cease to exist; yet the existence of my soul is eternal.

Down the hill from the clearing, the chapel bells rang in the hour. Whenever I hear church bells ringing, they take me back to the days of my youth on Donegal Hill. From my grandmother's home on Elm Street at the dusk of each day, I could hear the bells and chimes of different churches throughout the city. I always remembered those sunsets on Elm Street and the peace and serenity the bells and chimes instilled in me at the end of the day. Growing up in my Elm Street neighborhood, I always wanted to be part of a perfect family. On my grandmother's TV, I used to watch *Father Knows Best* and *Ozzie and Harriet,* anticipating that someday I would become a perfect father in a perfect family. I believed that it was part of God's plan for humanity that we all should be born into and participate in a perfect family throughout our lives. At least that is my perception of how things were supposed to be for everyone before things went wrong in the Garden of Eden.

Just as things in the Garden of Eden didn't work out, neither did they work out for me according to my plan. Somewhere along the elusive path of life, I lost touch with that goal of a perfect family life. Being the child of an alcoholic made it difficult for me to understand how a functioning family works. Becoming an active alcoholic myself didn't make me an ideal candidate for raising a family either. Certainly, getting into the nightclub business was not the direction for a family man. And if the statistics are correct, as a survivor of a near-death experience I am not exactly an ideal mate. I imagine that it is not too romantic to sit across the dinner table from a spouse who seems to be light years away in his thoughts, or spends time outdoors at night staring up at the stars and dreaming. I did not come back from my near-death experience as a perfect man. I did not come back as a saint. I just came back as much less of a sinner.

CHAPTER 25

BEST LAID PLANS

On Sunday morning, May 26, 1996, I left Club Marakesh at approximately 2:35 A.M. It was one of the few nights that I went to the club in several years, but I had come to say goodbye to many friends and employees who were saddened by the club's closing. I was not saddened; I couldn't be happier. On the following day, Club Marakesh was scheduled to close forever after twenty years of successful operation. At the same time, a group of new owners would occupy the premises to begin the renovations for the opening of a new club. My dream-come-true was only twenty-four hours away—I thought, but in less than two hours, the dream would turn into a nightmare due to circumstances beyond my control. As I was walking away from the building, I had an uneasy feeling that somehow things were not going to go my way.

As I left the club, a group of thugs remained behind, planning and scheming to create an incident that would disrupt the planned transition of the premises to new operators. Twenty minutes after the club closed for the night, a young black man was assaulted in the village's municipal parking lot by a group of white males. Witnesses stated that there were five or six assailants, two of them brandishing small handguns which they pointed and waved at everyone, threatening to shoot, while the victim was beaten in the head by one of the perpetrators with a metal club. Although the beating took place in a municipal lot that was usually patrolled by the police after the club closed, the village police were conspicuously missing. Security personnel leaving Club Marakesh came to the victim's aid and administered first aid, miraculously keeping the victim from bleeding to death. The security personnel also attempted to block the assailants' car from speeding away and they were almost run over by the gun-wielding thugs. The victim was airlifted to a major medical center where he underwent surgery and remained in a coma.

For several days, I went to the shrine and prayed for the young man who was lying unconscious in the hospital. The initial prognosis was poor for his either surviving or recovering. Although both the assailants and the victim had been patrons of the club prior to the attack, the incident had happened in the parking lot after the club had closed for the night without incident. Therefore, I had no reason to suspect that this incident would affect the transfer of the liquor license to the new tenants. Several days later, a New York City narcotics detective was arrested for being involved in the beating. As it turned out, it was his car in which the assailants fled, and the club's security personnel had provided the police with the license plate number that led to his arrest.

The arrest of a New York City police officer in what was being described as a bias-related beating of the young black man resulted in a media invasion of the

Hamptons. Satellite TV trucks from every major network including ABC, CBS, Fox, NBC, and CNN descended on the village and camped out in the municipal parking lot where the incident had occurred. The TV cameras focused their lenses on the entrance to Club Marakesh across the street, and reporters broadcast live reports anticipating the arrests of additional New York City policemen. When several more arrests were made, it was reported that the narcotics detective's accomplices were not police officers but individuals who had connections to organized crime.

As a result of the media attention, the politicians began to look for a scapegoat, portraying the already-closed Club Marakesh as a trouble spot and a rowdy bar, even falsely inferring that the incident had actually started earlier inside the nightclub. The mayor of New York City needed a scapegoat because a New York police officer was involved in the beating. The village officials needed a scapegoat because its police department failed to patrol the municipal parking lot, and they prevailed on the governor to interfere with the transfer of the liquor license to the new tenants.

The victim regained consciousness and survived the beating. However, my business and personal reputation that I had worked so hard to improve was suddenly ruined. The governor's interference with the liquor licensing of the nightclub prevented me from realizing a profitable business deal with the new tenants, the nightclub remained closed, and the building went into foreclosure. My real estate business began to suffer from the bad publicity; many of my salespeople went to work for competitors; and I was forced to sell my real estate business for a fraction of what it was worth prior to the beating incident. My home also went into foreclosure and I was forced to sell it at a reduced price with most of the proceeds going to pay debts and taxes. Finally, I had to declare personal bankruptcy. Despite my best efforts to convert my material possessions into cash assets while embarking on a more spiritual path, my planning did not work out the way I wanted it. I had been stripped of all my personal possessions just as I had been shown would happen during my NDE years before. My losses did not deter me from pursuing a spiritual path. I knew that my efforts would be rewarded in the end, but perhaps not in this world.

When I lost my home and businesses in the Hamptons, I spent several years traveling, particularly to Florida where I attempted unsuccessfully to return to a life of business ventures, and to California where I spent a period of time at the New Camaldoli Monastery high in the mountains overlooking Big Sur. I lived there in a simple, one-room cottage located on a hillside with a view looking out over the Pacific Ocean. I felt as close to heaven as I could get on earth, and I worked on the manuscript that would eventually become this book. I could never establish roots in the various places that I traveled because I knew that I was not going to advance along my spiritual path and perform my mission in life until I found the mountain and valley setting that I was shown in the future visions.

I moved on with my life, continued my research and writing, and became involved in the pro-life movement. In March 1997, I received a late Monday night call from Sarah Hinze, the author of *Coming From The Light*. Sarah had pioneered the research in pre-birth studies, compiling accounts of people, including herself, who had spiritual encounters with their yet-to-be-conceived or -born children. Sarah had been invited to Washington, D.C., to speak to a group of congressional leaders two days later during the House Judiciary Committee hearings on partial-birth abortion. Sarah asked me to join her and near-death experiencer Ranelle Wallace, author of *The Burning Within,* and to make a presentation. I immediately accepted, even though I had less than two days to prepare. I knew that another future vision was about to become reality. I met Sarah and Ranelle in Washington on Wednesday morning. We made our presentations before a group of congressmen in the Longworth Building during a recess in the partial-birth abortion debate. The personal stories Ranelle and I shared with the congressmen confirmed for them the information that Sarah had compiled in her study: that the soul is eternal, existing both before and after Earth life, that we all live as spirit children of God in a heavenly home before coming to earth, and that aborted children's souls are blocked and turned back from their mission.

During the presentation, I addressed the congressmen while dressed in a conservative business suit, just as I had been shown thirteen years before in my future life visions.

PART III

THE FUTURE

The wise shall shine brightly
like the splendor of the firmament,
And those who lead the many to justice
shall be like the stars forever.

Daniel 12:3

CHAPTER 26

THE FUTURE

"I will pour out My Spirit on all mankind.
Your sons and daughters shall prophesy,
your old men shall dream dreams,
your young men shall see visions.
Even upon the servants and the handmaids,
in those days, I will pour out My Spirit."

Joel 2:28–29

For ten years, the information from my near-death experience concerning visions of the End Times was stored in my memory, like a time capsule. During that time, I did not feel inspired to actively pursue validating my experience, justifying it, or attempting to parallel my experience with the experiences of others. It was not until I received the "phone call from heaven" in 1994 that I began to seriously research and investigate near-death experience phenomena and the meaning of my future visions.

I began my research by contacting Dr. Bruce Greyson, who was at the University of Connecticut at the time. Subsequently, Greyson took a position as professor of psychiatric medicine at the University of Virginia in Charlottesville in July 1995. As director of research for the International Association for Near-Death Studies, Dr. Greyson has become the preeminent leader in the research and study of near-death phenomena.

I had a dual purpose in meeting Dr. Greyson. First, I wanted to gather information in preparation for my research, and second, despite my lack of faith in certain aspects of the profession of psychiatry, particularly with the Freudian gang, I thought that it would be appropriate for me to seek professional consultation with Dr. Greyson. Remembering and reliving the course of events of my life and near-death experience in detail would prove to be a cathartic experience. I wanted to be certain that I remained on stable ground, emotionally and mentally, during the process. In addition to consulting with Dr. Greyson, I chose prayer, not Prozac, to achieve those results.

During the course of my meetings with Dr. Greyson, I elaborated on some of the personal and global visions of my near-death experience. Although my future visions of a global nature seemed unbelievable even to me, I learned that many other near-death experiencers throughout the world were coming back from the Other Side with the same or similar visions and messages. As an example, I was drawn to the story of a simple forester, Matous Lasuta. The following is an account of his story:

Matous Lasuta awoke on Sunday morning, June 1, 1958, in his small family cottage in the village of Turzovka in the mountains of Slovakia, a part of Czechoslovakia not far from the frontier of Poland. Matous had been a woodcutter, but in 1956 at the age of forty he was promoted to forester, a position of responsibility that required him to survey the forests near and around his village. On a typical Sunday, Matous and Eva, his wife, would gather their two daughters, nine-year-old Ann and three-year-old Teresa, and walk to Sunday services. Their oldest daughter, Mary, was already married and their first daughter had died tragically many years before; consequently, Sunday was always a day of remembrance. Sunday was also usually a day of rest for Matous following church attendance.

However, Matous was assigned to work on this particular Sunday. It was Matous's responsibility to survey the mountainous area called Okrouhla, which means "round mountain." At the top of this mountain was a lone pine tree that was well known to Matous and all the natives of the region, who called this place U-Obrazku, which means "the picture." This area was a favorite hiking destination for the local villagers, who traditionally stopped to say prayers at the base of the pine tree.

As Matous prepared to leave his cottage, he remarked to his wife: "How painful to be called to work, Eva! Sunday is not Sunday without church!"

Eva understood and shared this feeling, but she encouraged him: "Since it is your task to carry out a full day in the forest, you must accomplish it. Deprived of church on Sunday, yes, Matous, but don't forget that God is everywhere! You go where duty calls, but do not forget to stop for a moment of prayer at U-Obrazku!"

As Matous began his hike through the forest, he did so with deep regret for not being able to head in the opposite direction with his wife and two daughters to the church. Matous thought of himself as a simple man of the country, and despite having to work on Sunday he counted his blessings as he proceeded through the forest trail.

By nine o'clock, Matous had finished his hike and found himself at the clearing at U-Obrazku. Remembering Eva's advice, Matous knelt at the base of the lone pine tree and began to say a prayer to count his blessings. Matous had closed his eyes in prayer, but even with his eyes shut he suddenly sensed that an intense light surrounded him. Matous slowly opened his eyes, afraid that he would be blinded by the incredible light. As his eyes adjusted, he realized that the pine tree had disappeared, and he found himself in a beautiful flower garden. He doubted his senses for a moment, thinking that his sight was deceiving him, but then he thought he heard the voice of a woman calling to him. As he turned his head to look for the woman, he was astonished by the vision before him.

A Lady of Light stood suspended about one-half meter above the ground! The Lady of Light was surrounded by light, but the brilliance of the light that emanated from her was not from an earthly source. As Matous contemplated the vision of brilliant light before him, he was embarrassed by the visions, but he was consoled by the Lady of Light, and his uneasiness melted.

The Lady of Light extended her hand, and suddenly the beautiful flower garden vanished. Instead, Matous saw—as if in a movie—the terrestrial globe of planet Earth! As the scene unfolded before Matous, the Lady of Light remained silent. Yet the simple forester understood instantly that she was communicating an important message. He had no reason to question the message, knowing only that he had to absorb it. Matous understood that he was viewing what was going to happen to each of the individual countries—if the people in these countries did not return to God.

Matous perceived that some countries and regions were indicated in green, which meant that these countries and regions were in accordance with God's plan. But other countries and regions were indicated in yellow and were marked for destruction due to the unacceptable behavior of their people. Matous noticed that green areas were more abundant in the mountainous and therefore less populated regions, and that yellow areas dominated the more populated regions. He concluded that the people were less corrupted in the rural areas than in the populated ones.

Suddenly, the green areas of the land began to recede, and the yellow areas expanded and invaded into more and more areas and countries. Matous recognized that this surely meant the world was getting worse and worse. Soon, the yellow wave had invaded all the lands. Then powerful explosions burst forth suddenly over the water and over the land. A dense rain fell on the earth, the consistency of which Matous did not understand. When the rain reached the ground it burst into flames. Soon, all the areas touched by the rain were covered with fire. Then the visions ended and the Lady of Light suddenly disappeared.

Matous found himself alone in the forest at the base of the pine tree, trembling at the loss of the splendor of the bright light. He could hear the church bells ringing from the village and realized that it was 12:00 noon. The vision had lasted three hours.

Later that evening, a visibly shaken Matous Lasuta returned to his cottage in the village. Following the vision of the Lady of Light, he had spent much of the afternoon contemplating what had taken place. He decided to tell his wife about the appearance of the Lady of Light and the visions that he had been shown. His modest wife listened intently and responded in a supportive manner to the extraordinary events that were described to her by Matous.

Matous waited six days before returning to the site of the visions. If nothing happened on the return visit, he decided that he could assume that he had temporarily taken leave of his senses during the first visit. He thought that maybe he could even forget about the visions in time. But as Matous returned to the clearing and approached the lone pine tree, the brilliant light again surrounded him. The Lady of Light appeared again and continued to show Matous visions of the future of the world. Then she suddenly disappeared.

In all, the Lady of Light appeared to Matous six times during the summer months of 1958. On each of the appearances, the Lady of Light continued to show Matous visions of a troubled world urgently calling for the justice of God. The impending justice that was revealed to Matous Lasuta by the Lady of Light, however, was subject to a postponement, or even a cancellation, in the event that mankind returned to God.

The alternate visions presented to Matous revealed that two-thirds of humanity would be lost in a great cataclysmic event. The Sun would cease to be warm, and there would be cold summers with poor harvests. There would be terrible floods and other natural disasters. There would be earthquakes, and mountains would move into the oceans. Churches would collapse, and houses would be destroyed and carried away by floods. The nonbelievers would blaspheme in their despair. The air would be filled with demon-like forms, representative of sins and vices. These phantom forms would terrify humanity!

Then nature would calm down, and a bright light would appear—but the world would not be recognizable. Everything would be destroyed. It would be difficult to find human life or other living things.

The Lady of Light chose Matous to carry the message of the visions to all the people he could reach. Soon word spread about Matous and his visions to save the world, and the people, anxious to hear more, came to visit him.

On Sunday, September 8, 1958, Matous brought a group of people to *U-Obrazku*. The Lady of Light appeared to Matous and told him to convey to the people that her messages must be made known to the world and that prayer was the only salvation of the world. The people were puzzled by a final message from Matous: "In three days, I will leave you!"

On the following Wednesday, Matous was arrested and jailed by the police at the direction of the Communist officials. At his trial, Matous Lasuta was declared insane and confined in a mental institution in Byaritz, Sillein. After ten months of this humiliation, he was released. He then returned frequently to the site of the visions. But after another year, as more and more people came to visit him at U-Obrazku, he was arrested again by the Communist party and condemned to three more years of imprisonment.

Even though Matous was imprisoned, more and more people came to the site at U-Obrazku, so the Communist officials had the lone pine tree cut down, and then they burned and destroyed the entire area. Yet the pilgrims kept coming.

Matous, languishing in jail, had no regrets. Although he missed Eva and his daughters, he knew that he had to bear witness to the messages given to him by the Lady of Light. He had been chosen by the Lady of Light to deliver messages to the world and he knew that he was not alone. He remembered vividly one message the Lady of Light had delivered to him that assured him that he was not alone:

"Chosen ones will fall into a death-like sleep, but they will be protected by the angels! These chosen ones will be instructed by the angels on how to conduct themselves. They will be without any kind of fear during the most difficult hours. They will be protected by the good spirits, and they will be fed by heaven from where they will receive further instructions. When they awake from the death-like sleep, they will be as if newly born!"

What could a hedonistic and materialistic nightclub owner in the Hamptons in the 1980s have in common with a humble forester in a Communist country in the 1950s? What we had in common was the fact that we both had mystical experiences with similar messages from the same source of inspiration, the Lady of Light.

The one message to Matous that spoke of "chosen ones" who "will fall into a death-like sleep" describes the many near-death experiencers who have returned from near-clinical death episodes with messages from heaven—and without any medical diagnosis to explain what had happened to them.

Since Matous Lasuta received this message from the Lady of Light in 1958, this prophecy already has been and continues to be fulfilled throughout the world as people from all races, colors, religions, and beliefs are being brought back from the point of death with messages from heaven. These survivors no longer fear death, and as they resume their lives they feel as if they are newly born while they continue to receive further messages. They experience a spiritual awakening that continues to develop and unfold as their lives progress in a direction that manifests a message of love of God, self, and others, and service to mankind. But many of these survivors and other visionaries and seers are also coming back with messages of ominous proportions concerning the future of the world.

Why are we getting these messages from heaven? Why are people around the world coming back from "death" with similar experiences and future visions? Why are these survivors of death being spiritually transformed? Is God, through His angels and saints, now trying to communicate with us more directly? Does the phenomenal increase in near-death experiences foreshadow a future global spiritual transformation for all of humanity? Are these messages and experiences real?

For me, the messages and experiences are real and true. The reality of my experience is that many of my personal future visions have already occurred without my influence or control:

1. The Lady of Light showed me that I would put aside my business interests and materialistic pursuits and embark on a lifelong quest for truth and knowledge, beginning by my researching and writing about my experiences. Although I knew how to write prior to my near-death experience, I had no plans or desire to write a book. Certainly, I could not have written this manuscript myself without a lot of spiritual inspiration.

2. During my "death," I was shown a scene of me standing in a university auditorium conducting a seminar for an audience of doctors, medical researchers, and students. I relived this scene on August 4, 1995, when I actually addressed the North American Conference of the International Association for Near-Death Studies (IANDS) at the University of Hartford in Connecticut. It was the same auditorium and audience that I had been shown in the vision during my near-death experience eleven years before, on the evening of July 2, 1984.

3. During my near-death experience, I saw myself becoming involved in the film industry, specifically watching myself involved in the direction of movie scenes from my real-life experiences. A film and television executive producer from New York City traveled to Hartford, inspired to attend my seminar in anticipation of hearing my life story. With his encouragement, I began working on projects involving a feature film with a major studio and a television series with a national network.

4. During my near-death experience, I was told that I would be involved in communicating with the media. As a result of my work with IANDS and my presentation in Hartford, I was offered and accepted a position on the Board of Directors of IANDS as media spokesperson.

5. I watched scenes of my being at the bedside of sick and dying people. Shortly after my near-death experience, I began to perform hospice work, mostly by inspiration. Subsequently, I attended a hospice-training program and became a volunteer in my local community.

6. During my experience, I saw myself traveling extensively while writing and conducting seminars. In fact, I spent much of the past several years traveling to do research and to give seminars about the IANDS organization and my near-death experience. In the future, I plan to continue this work.

7. I was shown that much of my traveling would involve expeditions to the ruins of ancient civilizations. I plan to return to Egypt knowing that many of the mysteries concerning future events in our world will be found in

the clues that have been left by ancient civilizations in Egypt and at other locations.

The Lady of Light showed me global future visions as well as visions of my future personal life. Since many of the personal visions have already come true, I now believe, with confidence and concern, that the future global visions must be taken seriously. In fact, some of them have already occurred, and there is strong, supporting evidence that other future global visions may also become a reality.

1. When the Lady of Light first began to speak to me about the future of the world, I was shown that major events would happen first in the Middle East and then in Italy. I was told that these events would be acts of "aggression, terrorism, and war, performed by self-proclaimed radical groups, supposedly in the name of God." I now believe that the prophesies concerning the Middle East have begun to be fulfilled by the assassination of Israeli Prime Minister Yitzhak Rabin by a religious fanatic who claimed he was instructed by God to assassinate Rabin. I spoke about this vision during my seminar in Hartford on August 4, 1995, months before Rabin was assassinated.

2. I believe that a similar terrorist type attack will occur in the future in Italy, specifically in Rome. I believe that a fanatical religious group on a much larger scale will conduct the attack although it will be directed against one world leader. The focus of the attack will be upon the Vatican and the Papacy.

3. Terrorist attacks and acts of war and aggression will continue to plague the Middle East, Africa, and

Europe, as evidenced by the ethnic cleansing of Bosnia-Herzegovina. Many of these acts will be performed by religious fanatical terrorist organizations, supposedly in the name of God, but the Lady of Light told me that these acts of terrorism and war were never part of God's plan. In reality, these acts of aggression and war are the products of evil men who are motivated by power and greed, not love of God. They use God and religion as a cover to enforce their diabolical plans to ferment political turmoil and to enslave and control others.

4. Wars and rumors of war will continue to plague the Eastern Hemisphere, spreading from the Middle East into Africa and Europe, and then to countries of the former Soviet Union and to the Far East, particularly China.

5. The greatest threat to global peace and preservation will come from China, which is preparing itself for global war and domination by building the largest army in the world, prophetically referred to in the book of Revelation as the army of "two hundred million." Under the guise of population control, China has been systematically exterminating unborn female babies in favor of males in order to breed an army capable of dominating the world. The Lady of Light specifically told me, "Pray for the conversion of China. The conversion of China to God is necessary for the salvation of the world."

6. While acts of terrorism and war and political unrest plague the Eastern Hemisphere, the Western Hemisphere will be spared the worst of the terrorism. However, a major terrorist attack may befall New

York City or Washington, D.C., severely impacting the way we live in the United States.

7. The Western Hemisphere will be plagued mainly by natural disasters. Freakish, erratic, and unseasonable weather patterns will create severe tidal flooding and land erosion. There will be devastating tornadoes and wind storms; severe winter conditions with record snow falls and freezing temperatures; record summer heat waves with severe drought; and an increase in destructive storms and hurricanes.

8. The financial and banking institutions will collapse due in large part to the failure of the insurance companies as a result of the natural disasters. The United States will be thrown into political, economic, and social chaos.

9. The United States government will fail to meet its financial obligations as a result of its staggering national debt and will collapse. As a result of the destruction of U.S. military bases from natural disasters, the United States will lose its ability to wage war or defend itself, leaving the country vulnerable to invasion by foreign troops, particularly by China's "army of two hundred million."

10. Shadowy and publicly-unknown world figures will attempt to establish a "new world order" by creating a worldwide government supposedly for the benefit of humanity. As a group, they will attempt to reorganize the world's financial and banking institutions in a manner that will permit these unelected leaders to manipulate and control the future of the world for their own personal benefit and gain. Their

own personal greed and lust for material wealth and power will motivate them. They will attempt to create a secular and materialistic world devoid of individual freedoms.

11. A shifting of Earth's axis will create dramatic climatic changes and possibly result in massive earthquakes, volcanic eruptions, and huge tidal waves on both the east and west coasts of the United States, as well as around the world.

12. There will be a great shift in the location of populated areas as a result of both the geophysical and geopolitical changes. Coastal and other low-lying and unstable areas will diminish in population, while mountainous and other stable areas become more desirable. Spiritually-minded people will be drawn together to create new self-supporting and self-sustaining communities. These pioneers of vision who are attuned to God's plan for mankind will be the architects for the brave new world that God has envisioned for our future.

Although many of these future visions have already taken place or are now occurring, it is my belief that significant geopolitical and geophysical changes will continue to occur over the next several years. It is my further belief that the critical period of transition and change will be completed prior to the year 2034. Although these dates are based on visions I was shown during and following my near-death experience, I am reluctant to defend the accuracy of the timing for several reasons: First, only God knows with any certainty the course of human events and the future of our world and universe. Second, I returned from my near-death episode challenged in my ability to discern various elements of time and space. This characteristic phenomenon of many near-death survivors accounts for the fact that I originally perceived, incorrectly, that my near-death visions were to occur shortly after my return from death in 1984. Authors of the Bible and other prophets have experienced similar difficulties in perceiving the timing of events, some of them, for instance, believing that their prophetic visions of the End Times were to be fulfilled during their own lifetimes several thousand years ago.

Third, and most importantly, as the Lady of Light told me, "None of these events in the future need to take place if mankind begins to recognize and work with God's plan." A similar message was revealed to Matous Lasuta by the Lady of Light who told him that future events would be subject to "alleviation, or postponement, or even an abrogation in the case of a due return of mankind to God."

Will God interfere with our self-created destiny? Will God in His infinite mercy stop the terrorists from attacking, the armies from moving, the volcanoes from erupting, the earthquakes from rumbling, or the tidal waves from coming? Will we be worthy of His mercy? Will God give us another chance?

At this very moment, God is giving us the opportunity to change the course of events during these End Times, and the Holy Spirit, God's energy of love and knowledge, is being bestowed upon humanity with incredible magnitude. God is giving each of us the opportunity to open up our hearts and souls to Him. He is giving us the opportunity to let Him ignite the flame of His Spirit within each of us. Then we may individually arise to a level of spiritual transformation to communicate directly with God and to hear His message.

From the beginning of the creation of our souls, we have been given the capacity to find God within ourselves by giving Him the opportunity to ignite the flame in us—a flame that now may be only a flicker of light. Through this flame, our bodies and souls become filled with His Spirit which is our path to eternal light and salvation.

Many of us have already heard God's calling and are living in preparation for the final stages of the End Times. Many others have not answered His call and are living in darkness. However, God has prepared His plan for the future of all of mankind, and it includes:

1. A Global Spiritual Awakening. This event will be unparalleled in the history of humanity. It will be a worldwide spiritual and supernatural event that will be experienced by each and every individual soul living on the face of the Earth. Throughout the world, each individual soul will experience an inner awareness of the reality of God, Our Creator. Each and every person will experience a review of his or her own life and ask, "What have I done with my life? Where is my life going? What have I done to show love of God, love of my neighbor, and love of self? What have I done to be of service to mankind?"

2. A Protective Mantle upon the Earth. In God's own words: "I will pour out My Spirit on all of mankind!" (Joel 2:28). Following the Spiritual Awakening, God will continue to bestow His Spirit upon humanity. Every living soul will have the continuing opportunity to recognize and accept the gift of the Holy Spirit and to incorporate God into his or her life. Those who live in the light of God will continue to grow in spirit. Those who live in darkness will turn away from the light and fall further into darkness.

3. Miracles and Healings. An unprecedented number of miraculous and supernatural events will occur throughout the world, particularly beatific visions and apparitions. Healers who are filled with the Holy Spirit will perform miraculous healings, both spiritual and physical.

4. Cataclysmic Events. Depending on mankind's response to God, these events may be altered, postponed, or cancelled.

How are we to respond to God? Through prayer and meditation, we will begin to recognize and work with God's plan. As I was told by the Lady of Light, "The way to understand and work with God's plan is through prayer and meditation, through prayer to call to God, and through meditation to receive His message and His inspiration."

Prayer is the most powerful weapon in the arsenal of humanity. Prayer will arm us with the power to suspend the natural laws to avoid geophysically cataclysmic events. Geopolitical events can and will be influenced by the power of prayer. The future of the world can and will be determined not by its leaders but by the prayers of groups of people throughout the world. Prayer is the answer, not only around the world, but also in our country, in our homes, and in our hearts. The prayers of the people could save the world from war and destruction!

Alcohol, drugs, and other stimulants have become the choices that mankind has adopted to medicate and mask the pain that originates in the soul. However, it is prayer that provides the nourishment that heals our souls. Only prayer, not pills, can ultimately cure the anxiety of the soul. The miracle of prayer is that it works through the pain and discovers the source, which is an unresolved conflict within the soul. If we each, individually and collectively, find and deal with the conflicts within our souls, we will come closer to discovering our mission in life and God's plan for us.

The future of the world rests in our hands. The right choice is obvious. If each and every individual aspires to lead a life of love of God, self, and neighbor, collectively mankind has the ability to determine the future of the world and to choose our destiny as a civilization. Individually, we have the responsibility to do our part to achieve a future for mankind that is in accordance with God's plan. It is not for us to question whether or not God will allow cataclysmic events to devastate humanity. If the future of the world is doomed, it is of our own making. It must be a determination for us, individually and collectively, to change the course of events. God is making Himself available to us through His Holy Spirit to give us the courage, strength, and wisdom to change the course of future events for the betterment of mankind.

EPILOGUE

Since my NDE, I have been drawn to an area I identify as "Sugarloaf," located several miles outside of Hazleton. Each time I visited this mountain and valley area in the past, I visualized what had been shown to me as the future of this area, and each time the future visions seemed implausible. I thought perhaps that I was really not looking in the right area, but I kept trying because I knew that it was important for me to find this future place in my life before I could move on with my spiritual mission.

In the summer of 1999, I decided to return to Hazleton again in search of "Sugarloaf"; only this time, I drove south from Sugarloaf Mountain into a different mountain and valley area on a beautiful summer day. Although I had spent the first eighteen years of my life living only six miles from this new mountain and valley area, I was not aware of its existence when I was growing up. At that time, it was a primitive and undeveloped area. Since then a winding two-lane road has been constructed from the mountaintop down through the valley. When I drove down this road, I was "drawn" to pull over at a clearing on the side of the mountain. I was overcome with joy when I recognized that the scene before me was the mountain and valley view that I had seen in my future visions, exactly fifteen years before. I knew that I had found my new future home on earth. This was confirmed for me when I identified the location on a map. A nearby mountain was labeled Little Sugarloaf Mountain. During my NDE, I had been shown this area as a "safe place" to live in the future. I also believed it was to become the location for the Mission of Angels Foundation and the country inn that I knew would be part of my future. When I am not traveling, I now spend part of my time in this mountain and valley area.

I'm now expanding the goals of the Mission of Angels Foundation. Many individuals, angels if you will, have fallen into place and are assisting me in this work. I don't have the financial resources that I had planned to bring to "Sugarloaf" with me, but I now recognize that God provides me with what I need, not necessarily what I want. And that's okay with me. The superficial trappings that were part of my materialistic existence in places like the Hamptons and Palm Beach no longer concern me.

At the top of a nearby mountain there is a large outcropping of rock. This is the highest point in this area of northeastern Pennsylvania, approximately twenty-two hundred feet above sea level. I frequently visit this high point of the mountain, particularly at sunrise and sunset. There is a view over the nearby valleys, lakes, and mountaintops that goes on for miles. It is an ideal place for meditation and contemplation, and sometimes even speculation.

I no longer speculate about the future visions concerning my personal life, because many of them have already become reality, and I now spend part of my time in the mountain and valley area where much of my future life will unfold. On the basis of my personal future visions becoming reality, I sometimes speculate that the geopolitical and geophysical changes will also eventually become reality. Many of these changes have already begun or are already taking place. However, the global changes that may occur are too ominous to ponder, if they are to become reality. The visions that I had been shown concerning massive coastal flooding could be accelerated by the process that we now recognize as global warming, which has already created flood conditions in certain coastal areas around the world. If the process continues to accelerate, many more people will be drawn to move to "safe places" in the mountains to avoid the coastal flooding.

I do speculate that one of the most catastrophic events would be the shifting of Earth's axis. In such an event, surviving on planet Earth, even in the more secure mountainous areas, would be next to impossible. Although a shifting of Earth's axis seems inconceivable, there is credible evidence that it has shifted in the past, and on more than one occasion. I sometimes speculate that the future visions concerning a shifting of Earth's axis are actually symbolic of a mass shifting of consciousness that would bring humanity closer to God. I believe this will happen during the End Times, but it is also possible that such an event will be accompanied by great cataclysmic events. The message from the Archangel Michael forewarns of such cataclysmic events, if mankind does not return to God. Perhaps I should not speculate further.

I still spend much of my time in the Hamptons where Ginnie lives with our son, Michael, and his first cousin Jacob. Michael and Jacob are the same age, and I'm helping Ginnie with parenting both of them. Of all the experiences of my life, the joy of being Dad is the greatest of all. The most important lesson that I learned on the Other

Side is the importance of bringing children into the world. They are our spiritual brothers and sisters who are waiting in God's world to be born into the realm of this world. It is our relationship with our children and our experiences with them that give us our closest connection to God.

One of those experiences happened in Michael's short life when he was just two years old. Perhaps all parents have experienced that feeling that no matter how much one tries to protect one's children, things will go wrong and happen when they are going to happen. Some of the greatest lessons of life are learned during those moments.

It was a beautiful summer day when I unlatched a gateway on the protective fence surrounding the pool. I was momentarily distracted moving the pool furniture and organizing things when Michael slipped quietly behind me and toddled down the side of the pool to the deepest end. I can still remember that feeling. It was a sickening feeling that came over me as I was moving a chair. Suddenly I was frozen to the spot; I felt as if a part of my soul had been torn away from me. It was one of those moments in life when time and space seem to stand still.

Something was missing! As I turned toward the pool, I watched helplessly as Michael, seemingly in slow motion, stumbled and fell into the deepest end of the pool. I ran and then I dove and swam to the bottom of the pool to the deepest point where Michael's body had quickly sunk. I instinctively knew from lifeguard training that his lungs must have filled with water, as he sank like a stone. As I reached down for his body, I noticed how he seemed to be floating peacefully at the bottom of the pool, his arms and legs extended out strongly but motionless.

As I wrapped my arm around his body and propelled us both to the surface, I applied pressure with my hand beneath his chest cavity and pressed down to remove the water from his body. As we broke the surface, I watched as a stream of water gushed from his mouth.

His face was radiant with an expression as if he had just experienced a wonderful event. When the water was finally purged and he began to breathe heavily, his eyes were beaming and his mouth formed a large O shape.

I was amazed at how much strength I mustered at that moment as I held Michael with one arm and lifted us both out of the water with one swift motion of the other arm. I knew that he was okay, but I'll never forget the first words he mumbled: "Daddy! What was that?"

A year and a half later, Michael and I were returning from a U.S. Marine Corps Reserve Center, where we had delivered several truckloads of toys for the "Toys for Tots" program. On the way home, Michael and I stopped at a roadside stand and bought our Christmas tree. After securing the tree across the roof of the Jeep wagon, I drove east down the highway to our home in the Hamptons. The sun was setting in the west as a full moon rose on the horizon at the end of the highway directly in front of us. It seemed as if we could have driven right up to it. I continued driving, glancing at Michael and watching as the moonbeams bounced off his rosy cheeks.

"Daddy, do you remember when I drowned in the pool?" I was shocked that Michael was recalling this incident. He had not mentioned it before in the year and a half since that day.

"Yes, I remember, Michael, but I am surprised that you remember it."

"Remember, Daddy, I drowned and I died, but did I go to heaven?"

"No, Michael, you didn't die. You fell in the pool, and Daddy jumped in and pulled you out, but you didn't die."

"Yes, I did!" he was adamant. "I drowned, and I died!"

"And then what happened?" I responded, filled with curiosity.

"Well, when I drowned, and I died, a big, big fish came along, and he scooped me up and took me to a big flashlight in the sky."

"No, Michael," I said, "I scooped you up and saved you!" As I spoke, I realized what my son was trying to tell me, and I was denying him his experience.

"No, Daddy." He was very insistent. "I drowned, and I died! And the big, big fish scooped me up and took me to a big, big flashlight!"

I sat silent. Michael was describing his own near-death experience. And here I was, the near-death experience expert, trying to deny what he experienced.

We continued to drive in silence. It seemed as if we were driving right to the moon, which was still directly in front of us and brighter and larger than I have ever seen it. Finally, Michael broke the silence. "Daddy, when I died, I saw Grandpa. You know, the Grandpa Michael." Michael had never seen his Grandpa Michael before, at least not in this world. Grandpa Michael died in 1987, four years before Michael was born.

Another minute of silence. I was continually glancing at Michael as I drove, observing that he was obviously deep in thought. I knew that this was a special moment between a father and his son that I would remember for eternity.

Michael broke the silence again. "Daddy, isn't God wonderful?"

"He truly is," I responded. "He truly is."

AFTERWORD

According to the Gallup organization and other near-death research studies, an estimated thirteen million adults in the United States have reported having near-death experiences, and the number is growing.

Although similar experiences have been reported by many children, the total number of children's experiences is not yet known.

DO YOU HAVE A
SENSE OF MISSION?

Have you had a significant spiritual experience that has become a life-changing event for you? Has a friend or member of your family had an experience?

Spiritually transformational experiences are happening to people throughout the world more than at any other time in human history. These experiences include near-death experiences, pre-birth experiences, pre- and after-death visions, apparitions, interior locutions, miracles, and other spiritual phenomena.

The Mission of Angels Foundation is dedicated to gathering these experiences and sharing them with others who may also become inspired by what some people are experiencing. The Mission of Angels Foundation publishes a newsletter in which your experiences may be included.

If you would like to share your experiences with others and/or are interested in receiving the newsletters, please visit the author's website at: www.fastlanetoheaven.com or write to:

Ned Dougherty
P.O. Box 888
Hazleton, Pennsylvania 18201

If you are interested in arranging media interviews, or to have Ned Dougherty visit your group, please e-mail him at: ndened1@fastlanetoheaven.com

If you would like more information about the Mission of Angels Foundation, visit our website at: www.missionofangels.org or write to:

Mission of Angels Foundation
P.O. Box 888
Hazleton, Pennsylvania 18201

Please include a self-addressed, stamped business envelope and appropriate handling costs if you desire a response.

INDEX

efforts to control, 186
seeing other people's, 128
of the United States, 172-
174, 231
vision of personal, 75-76,
178-179, 185

gardening, therapeutic value
of, 190
Garth, Sir Samuel, 93
geophysical changes, vision
revealing, 78
Gibran, Kahlil, 139
global spiritual transformation, 249, 256
God
anger at, 168
answering call of, 256
communication with, 213
feeling embraced by, 24
listening to, 175
in the presence of, 34
thinking about, 13
wonderfulness of, 265
God's light
bringing to others, 144
feeling suspended in, 26,
203
God's plan, 28
failure to understand, 167
to radiate a life force
throughout the world, 89-
90
to spread gift of spiritual
sight, 127

for the United States, 173-
174
working with, 78-79, 257
going home, 113-124
golden light, 27, 42, 184,
214, 222
Greyson, Dr. Bruce, 181,
183, 241-242
guidance, 114, 121, 131, 140,
199, 259
guilt, 43

Hall of Records, 77
hallucinations. *See* apparitions
the Hamptons, 3-11
Heaven, phone call from,
199-204
"Heaven on Earth," 89
heavenly realms
Earth a part of, 73, 89
many levels of, 89
test of music from, 186-188
Hell, fear of, 41-42
Hinze, Sarah, 238-239
homecoming experience, 32-
33, 88, 90, 115
dreaming about, 232
Hopi concepts, 54
hospice work, 207, 250
the hospital experience, 94-
112
human body, a hindrance, 21
humanity
awakening, 78, 173
never alone, 121

ABOUT THE AUTHOR

 A graduate of St. John's University in New York, Ned Dougherty was a real estate broker for twenty-six years, the owner of two high-profile, successful nightclubs, and a spokesman and member of the board of directors for the International Association for Near Death Studies. Since his near-death experience (recounted in this book), Ned has worked towards fulfilling a goal he glimpsed in his visionary experience: to create a nonprofit organization called Mission of Angels and to assist in the creation of a new community of spiritually-minded people. He now divides his time between Pennsylvania and the Hamptons on Long Island, New York. *Fast Lane to Heaven* is his first book.

HAMPTON ROADS
PUBLISHING COMPANY, INC.

Thank you for reading *Fast Lane to Heaven*. Hampton Roads is proud to publish an extensive array of books on the topics discussed in *Fast Lane to Heaven*—topics such as near-death experiences, Virgin Mary apparitions, and more. Please take a look at the following selection or visit us anytime on the web: www.hrpub.com.

Eyes of an Angel
Soul Travel, Spirit Guides, Soul Mates, and the Reality of Love
Paul Elder

Following a near-death experience at the age of 41, a psychic doorway opened within Paul Elder and his ordinary life has never been the same. Passing repeatedly through that psychic doorway, Elder returned with a series of stunning revelations as to our true nature and purpose in the universe. A compelling, inspiring, and important book, *Eyes of an Angel* integrates near-death and out-of-body experiences in a way that has never been done before.

Paperback • 248 pages • ISBN 1-57174-429-0 • $15.95

www.hrpub.com · 1-800-766-8009

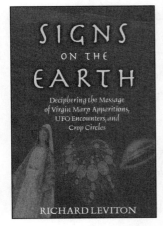

Signs on the Earth
Deciphering the Message of Virgin Mary Apparitions, UFO Encounters, and Crop Circles
Richard Leviton

Leviton examines the exploding number of paranormal reports from around the world and insists the signs indicate we're fast approaching the end of world as we know it—but that might not be such a bad thing. He believes that these phenomena are messages from the surrounding galaxy offering us an unprecedented opportunity to enter the next level of reality.

Paperback • 304 pages • ISBN 1-57174-246-8 • $15.95

Soul Journeys
My Guided Tours through the Afterlife
Rosalind A. McKnight

In Soul Journeys, McKnight relates her explorations of the afterlife with a being she calls Radiant Lady. With Radiant Lady as her spiritual guide, McKnight explores and reports on the non-physical energies in the afterlife. *Soul Journeys* reveals the inner workings of the other dimensions including the afterlife and emphasizes that all of us have spirit guides we can work with at any time.

Paperback • 272 pages • ISBN 1-57174-413-4 • $15.95

Cosmic Journeys
My Out-of-Body Explorations with Robert A. Monroe
Rosalind A. McKnight

Foreword by Laurie Monroe

Mcknight was one of the first and most successful out-of-body research explorers to work with Robert Monroe. In *Cosmic Journeys* she recounts the early days of The Monroe Institute and her sessions in the famed "black box."

Paperback • 296 pages • ISBN 1-57174-123-2 • $13.95

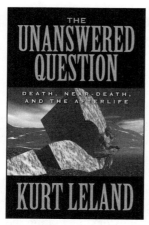

The Unanswered Question
Death, Near-Death, and the Afterlife
Kurt Leland

Seasoned astral traveler Leland explores the deepest reaches of consciousness in an attempt to answer the great question: Is a near-death experience the same as real death? What he finds will fascinate and enlighten you, and more importantly, convince you that everything you think you know about near-death may be dead wrong.

Paperback • 520 pages • ISBN 1-57174-299-9 • $16.95

Eternal Life and How to Enjoy It
A First-Hand Account
Gordon Phinn

This description of what happens after people die was transmitted directly from Henry, a fun-loving, care-free soul—who just so happens to be dead. Henry describes his "first day dead," the various heavens and hells, and his own experiences as an afterlife guide for the newly deceased. Most importantly, Henry reveals what awaits us all and demonstrates how our beliefs in this life create the reality we experience in the next.

Paperback • 224 pages • ISBN 1-57174-408-8 • $13.95

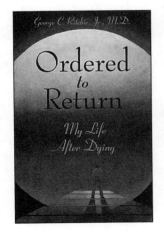

Ordered to Return
My Life After Dying
George G. Ritchie, Jr., M.D.

At age 20, as a private in the army, George Ritchie died of pneumonia. Nine minutes later, he came back profoundly changed. What he saw during those few minutes dead would change his life and the lives of his family and friends forever.

Paperback • 184 pages • ISBN 1-57174-096-1 • $12.95

Hampton Roads Publishing Company

. . . for the evolving human spirit

HAMPTON ROADS PUBLISHING COMPANY publishes books on a variety of subjects, including metaphysics, spirituality, health, visionary fiction, and other related topics.

For a copy of our latest trade catalog, call toll-free, 800-766-8009, or send your name and address to:

HAMPTON ROADS PUBLISHING COMPANY, INC.
1125 STONEY RIDGE ROAD • CHARLOTTESVILLE, VA 22902
e-mail: hrpc@hrpub.com • www.hrpub.com